KiCad 6
Brief introduction for the practitioner

KiCad 6

Brief introduction for the practitioner

Jörg Bischof
DM6RAC

The contents of this book have been created with great care. Nevertheless, the author cannot guarantee that the content is correct, up-to-date or complete. He is not liable for any damage that may result from the use of the information provided here. The circuits, programs and other information shown are for training purposes and are without regard to any patent claims. The software and hardware designations, brand names and product designations used in the book are the property of the companies concerned.

Copyright © 2022 Jörg Bischof
All rights reserved

ISBN: 9798361777655

Imprint: Independently published

Table of Contents

0	Introduction	6
1	General notes on the printed circuit board	10
	1.1 The circuit board	10
	1.2 The components	11
	1.3 Placement of the components	11
	1.4 Design of the conductors	13
2	Installation and configuration	16
	2.1 Installation	16
	2.2 The Project Manager	17
	2.3 Configuration	20
	2.4 Template	21
3	The Schematic	24
	3.1 Schematic Editor interface	24
	3.2 Set up schematic	26
	3.3 Drawing the schematic	27
4	PCB Editor	38
	4.1 PCB Editor interface	38
	4.2 Board Setup	44
	4.3 Routing	46
5	Fabrication Outputs	58
	5.1 Files needed	58
	5.2 Creation of the Gerber files	58
6	References	65
7	Index	66

0 Introduction

I've been tinkering with electronics since I was young. Of course, this also included printed circuit boards. In the past, the circuit board layout was designed with a pencil on small squared notepads or graph paper. In a grid of 2.5 mm. Which of course then led to problems with the advent of circuits in the 0.1" grid. The drawn layout was placed on the copper-clad board, scored with a scriber, then drilled. The drill holes were the orientation for drawing. Candle wax was used as a cover and the dividing lines scratched out. Etched with concentrated nitric acid. The nitrogen oxides were a terrible stench. Later there was iron-III-oxide to buy. Then nitro lacquer was applied with a tubular pen and etched with it. The many stains that were created and that were "real" were beautiful. Attempts were also made with waterproof fiber pen and etched with sodium persulphate.

Later you had a computer and the first layout programs came out. At first it was quite cumbersome: you had to write down a list of what was connected to whom. And the autorouters created adventurous layouts that could hardly be drawn. Printing and photochemical processes were hardly possible for the amateur.

Today there are good programs that can be used to design and print both the circuit diagram and the circuit board layout. There are providers who produce circuit boards professionally and you can use the programs to generate the necessary data.

I tried some programs: Autodesk Eagle, Target3001! and KiCad. It was also always important to me that I could use it to draw the circuit and that DIN EN 60617 was adhered to as far as possible. The latter is not always self-evident. Often either obsolete or US circuit symbols appear. I ended up befriending KiCad. Not least because I was able to install it on my Mac. In addition to macOS and Windows, there are download options for a number of Linux derivatives.

I would like to explain here the basic steps to be taken with the KiCad program. I am referring to version 6.0.4. A lot also applies to version 5 and will probably not change fundamentally with newer versions.

Not all possibilities should be exhausted. In addition, there are guaranteed to be thicker and more expensive books. I just want to show what you need in everyday life to design your circuit and circuit board and then ultimately either manufacture it yourself or have it manufactured by a service provider.

First, I'll give a few pointers to keep in mind when designing a circuit, then and based on that, lay out the board. There aren't too many rules and many are just logical. I'm assuming that we're not developing any projects with high tension or very high frequencies. There are special features that go beyond the normal amateur everyday life. I will explain the necessary steps to do this here. I also go into how you can expose circuit boards yourself and then produce them. Maybe one or the other trick will help to create a good product.

If you don't need a small circuit board quickly, you can have circuit boards professionally manufactured for very little money, provided you find a cheap service provider you trust. I also explain the necessary steps to do this. You don't have to fall into every trap...

I wish you a lot of fun and a lot of success.

Chapter 1
Printed circuit board

1 General notes on the printed circuit board

1.1 The circuit board

The printed circuit board (PCB) is the carrier of the electronic circuit. It can consist of different materials. It used to be laminated paper impregnated with phenolic resin (NEMA classification: FR2). Today, however, this material is considered obsolete.

A material that is easy to process mechanically is hard paper that is provided with epoxy resin as a binder. In the NEMA classification, the designation is FR3. Classification FR4 is the standard material. The carrier material is glass fabric, which is impregnated with epoxy resin. However, the latter places some demands on the drills. Carbide drill bits should be used for drilling. Ordinary drills dull very quickly.

One or two-sided circuit boards are common for the amateur. The circuit boards usually have a copper layer with a thickness of 35 µm. There are also circuit boards with a 17 µm and 70 µm thick copper layer. Later, if you want to expose and etch the board yourself, I recommend sticking to the dimensions specified by the manufacturer of the photo boards. Dividing the board before exposure is hardly possible and afterwards it requires work and unnecessary waste. If you take a service provider, the size usually only matters for the price.

It is difficult to make a make a feedthrough from one side to the other with amateurish means on two-sided boards. It is possible to use special tubular rivets with the associated pressing tools. However, the price of the tool is usually outside of what you want to spend on your hobby. The only alternative is to use connections from components or short pieces of wire.

1.2 The components

We differentiate between two major categories of components:

- Components for through-hole mounting (Through Hole Technology – THT).
  These are components that have connecting wires that are pushed through holes.

- Surface Mounted Technology (SMT) components.
  These are the so-called SMD components that are soldered directly onto the conductor track.

For components with axial wires as connections (resistors, chokes, etc.), it makes sense to get a bending gauge. It costs around one euro, but ensures that you have evenly curved connections. Later, when selecting the component, you decide on the distance between the connections.

I like to use SMD components in size 1206 or occasionally 0805 for capacitors and resistors. These can still be soldered reasonably well by hand. But they are nice and small and you don't have to drill any holes. Transistors and diodes as SMD are also feasible. With the "centipedes" it can get quite tight.

Circuits in the DIP package can be installed with or without a circuit socket. Transistors, LEDs, etc. should not sit directly on the circuit board, but should have a small distance. In this way, the heat generated during soldering can be kept somewhat away from the semiconductor crystal.

1.3 Placement of the components

Once you have decided on a certain size of circuit board, you place the components. The placement already determines how good or bad the conductor path management will be. In KiCad, so-called *air lines* indicate which connector is connected to which other. You can turn the components in such a way that there are few crossovers.

Before that, however, you have to think about placements that require certain locations. Above all, that would be:

- Location of controls located on the circuit board.

- Components that emit heat and components that are sensitive to heat should be spatially separated.

- Circuit parts that generate interference (e.g. switching power supplies) and sensitive circuit parts should be arranged in such a way that they do not affect each other.
  You should also keep an eye on the ground: return currents from current-intensive or fast-switching digital parts can affect sensitive parts (e.g. preamplifiers). Sometimes a separation into different ground areas makes sense. These are then connected to each other in a star configuration.

- At higher frequencies, RF considerations must then also be taken into account.

If there are several identical assemblies in one housing (e.g. gates or several operational amplifiers), an easier connection may be possible if similar connections (pin swapping) or the assemblies are exchanged with one another (gate swapping). Important: Always make sure that later the board layout and

Ladder width		Application	maximum current
[mm]	[mil]		[A]
0,35	14	standard width, conductor fits between two 2.54 mm (0.1 in) pitch connectors	1,0
0,91	36	if there is enough space	1,5
1,47	58		2,0
2,18	86	power supply	3,0
3,45	136	for power components and large capacitors	5

Tab. 1: Conductor path width

the circuit match. If possible, therefore, make changes in the circuit.

The components have a defined connection grid. This is defined in inches. For DIP circuits, for example, it is 2.54 mm (=1/10"). The connections of the components must of course also be located in this grid. In order to have more "freedom of movement", it makes sense to select the placement grid in such a way that it is an integer divisor of the connection grid.

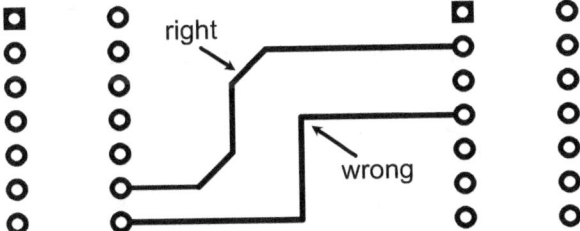

Fig. 1: Ladder guide

Fig. 2: Pads

1.4 Design of the conductors

An important characteristic of the ladder is its width. There isn't much you can do about the height. This is already defined with the copper thickness and is usually 35 µm. In addition to the available space, the following should be considered:

- The current-carrying capacity depending on the permissible heating.

- The resistance of the conductor.

- The inductive and capacitive influence of several conductors on each other.

- The technologically minimum conductor width that can be generated (take into account: during etching, the etching solution not only acts from top to bottom, but also sideways).

The width of signal and control lines is usually of secondary importance. The currents are pretty small here. This is different with power supply lines and supply lines to power stages.

Important conductor widths are listed in table Tab. 1 (I took it from [1] in abbreviated form).

For those who are not familiar with the unit mil:
1 mil = 1/1000 in = 0.0254 mm.

I use 0.35 mm and 0.5 mm for normal lines and 1.0, 1.5 and 2.0 mm for power lines. To minimize the capacitances, the narrowest possible conductor widths are recommended.

When laying the conductors, the wiring should be as short and straight as possible. Unnecessarily small distances should be avoided. Avoid acute angles. When laying cables, laying them at right angles may look good, but not for conductors on the printed circuit board. There is always a risk of reflections, hairline cracks or undercuts. Therefore bevel at an angle of 45° (Fig. 1).

It should be noted that the soldering points are clearly defined.

If a soldering point is on a larger area (e.g. ground), so-called heat traps must be provided. They prevent the surrounding copper surfaces from dissipating too much heat and thus making soldering difficult. In many cases it also makes sense to plan the free area as a copper area and to define it as ground.

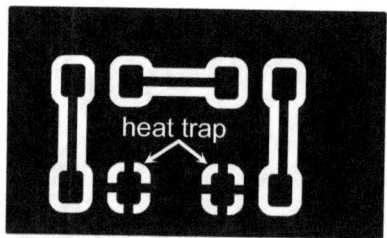

Fig. 3: Heat trap

Chapter 2
Installation and configuration

2 Installation and configuration

2.1 Installation

The screenshots are shown here in the German version. But the English one is analog to this one. In the text I give the English terms.

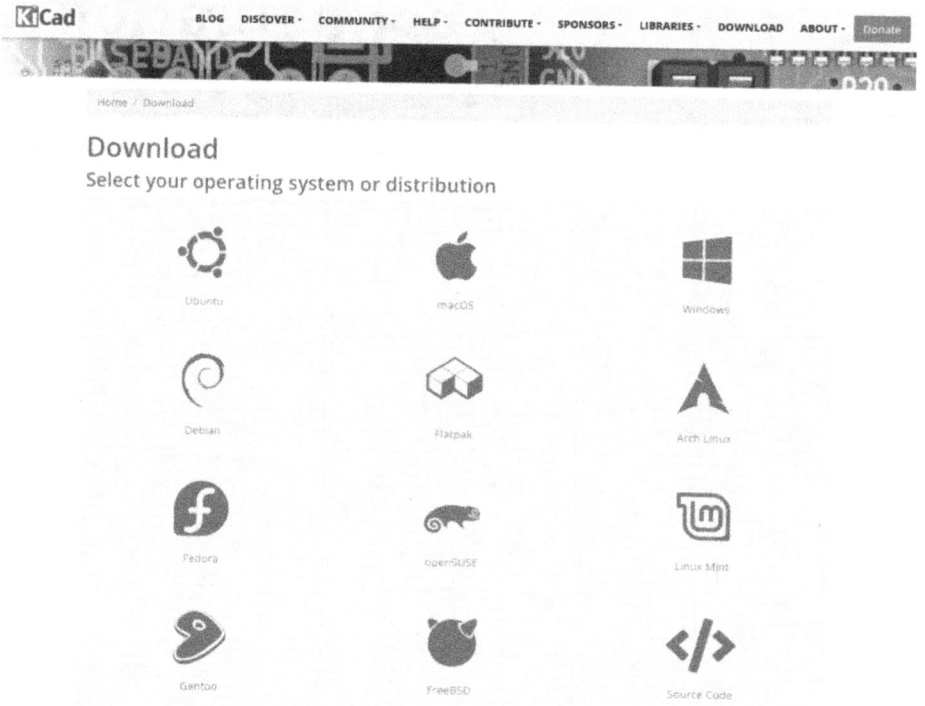

Fig. 4: Download KiCad

KiCad can be found at https://www.kicad.org/download It is available for different operating systems:

The installation takes place as usual. Depending on the operating system, libraries for the components, their footprints and symbols as well as templates are installed at different locations. I won't go into the exact locations now, because in practical application the exact location is not that important.

After installation, the program can be started. We start with the project manager. It manages all files that are required to create the circuit and then the circuit board. It makes sense to create a separate folder for each project.

2.2 The Project Manager

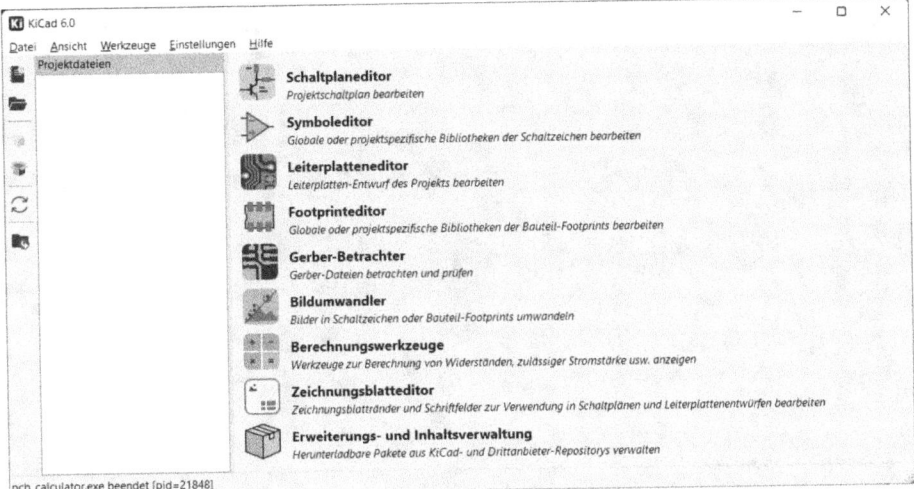

Fig. 5: The Project Manager

In the project manager, a new project can be created, existing projects can be opened and archiving can be carried out. All this via the left side of the window. You can see that a file for the circuit and one for the board has already been created. The project manager window always remains open. If it is closed, the program ends. The actual project file ends with *.kicad_pro. As soon as the circuit or board is processed, the backup is created immediately.

On the right side you can see more buttons:

- Schematic Editor:
  For editing the circuit diagram. Does the same thing when I double click on the *.kicad_sch file.

- Symbol Editor:
  The symbols (schematic diagrams) stored in the libraries are listed. They can be edited here.

Chapter 2: Installation and configuration

- **PCB Editor:**
  For processing the circuit board. Again, the same as double-clicking on *.kicad_pcb.

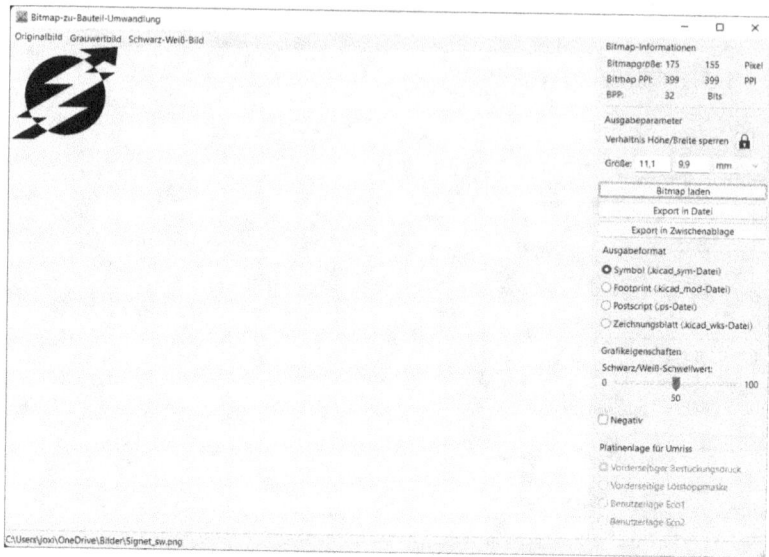

Fig. 6: Image Converter

- **Footprint Editor:**
  Similar to the symbol editor - only now the footprints of the components.

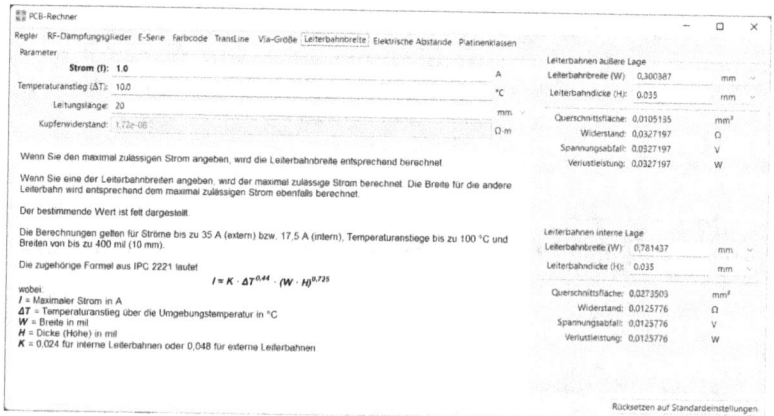

Fig. 7: Calculator Tools

- Gerber Viewer:
  Will be used later to view the Gerber files needed for printed circuit board (PCB) manufacturers.

- Image Converter:
  Here you can convert images into footprints. Interesting if logos etc. are to be inserted.

- Calculator Tools:
  This window contains interesting tools to calculate conductor widths, distances between conductors, attenuators, etc.

- Drawing Sheet Editor:
  Both circuit and board are drawn in a drawing sheet with labeling fields. With this editor this can be adjusted.

- Plugin and Content Manager:
  Third-party extensions can be installed. I definitely recommend the Interactive Html Bom extension. This allows you to create bills of materials and have the components displayed on a printed circuit board. And all this in the browser (an HTML file is generated).

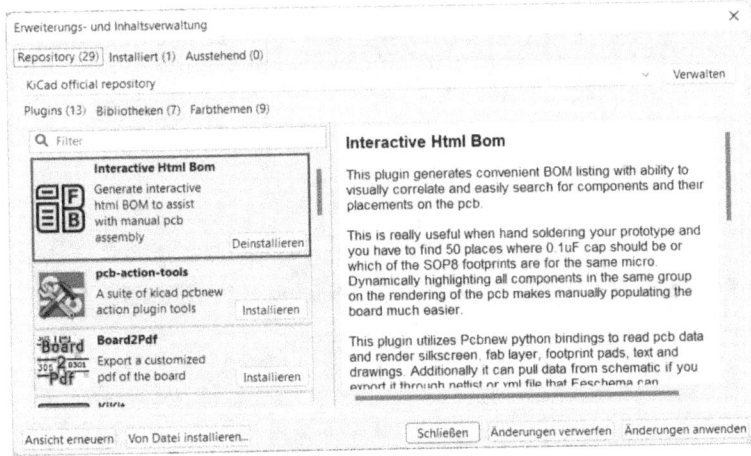

Fig. 8: Plugin and Content Manager

2.3 Configuration

In the settings, the appearance, the creation of backup copies, the behavior of the mouse and the keyboard shortcuts are set. I think the settings here are self-explanatory and need no further explanation.

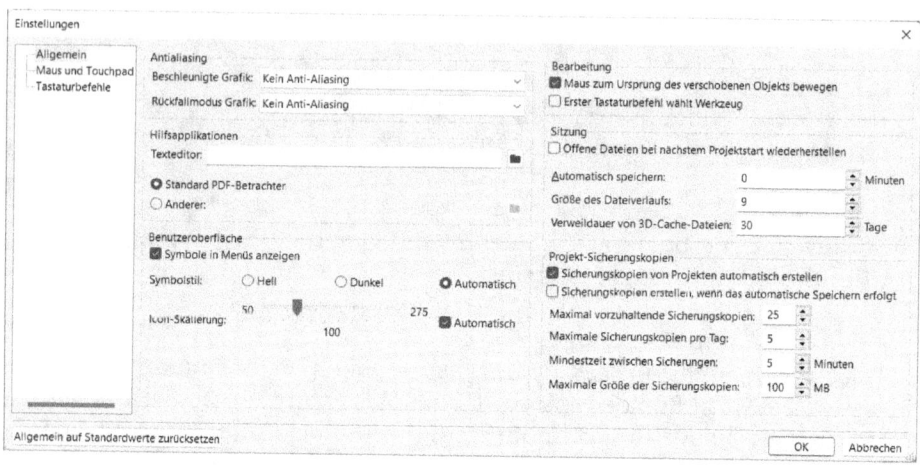

Fig. 9: Preferences

The *Preferences* → *Configure Paths* setting defines the locations where models, footprint, symbol, and template libraries reside. This affects both the installed libraries and your own. You can add your own (+) or delete existing ones (recycle bin). If you click in the path, the location can also be changed. But I think people will just leave the places where they are.

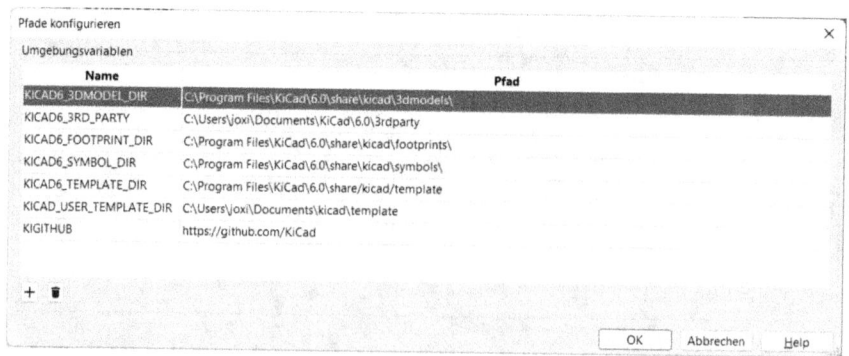

Fig. 10: Pfade

The symbol and footprint libraries can then be managed under *Preferences* → *Manage Symbol Libraries* and *Preferences* → *Footprint Libraries*. When first called up gives a hint how to configure it.

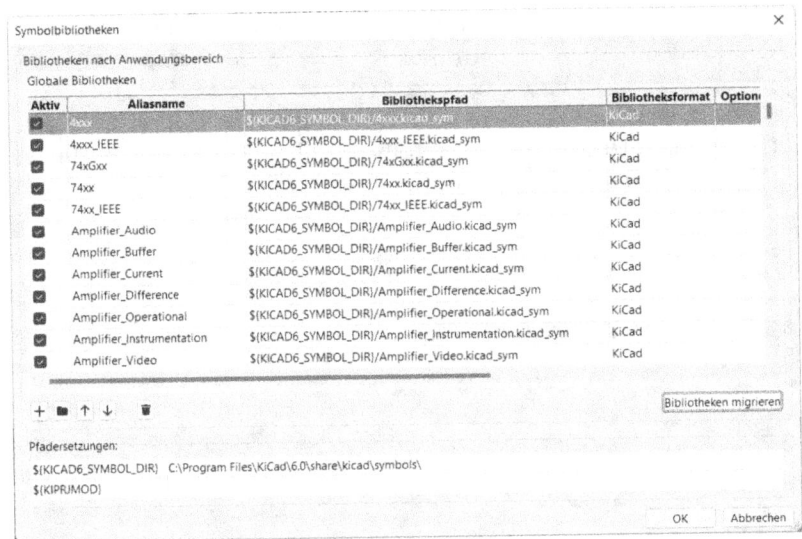

Fig. 11: Note configuration libraries

You can safely accept the default setting. The same window then appears when you call up the second library.

2.4 Template

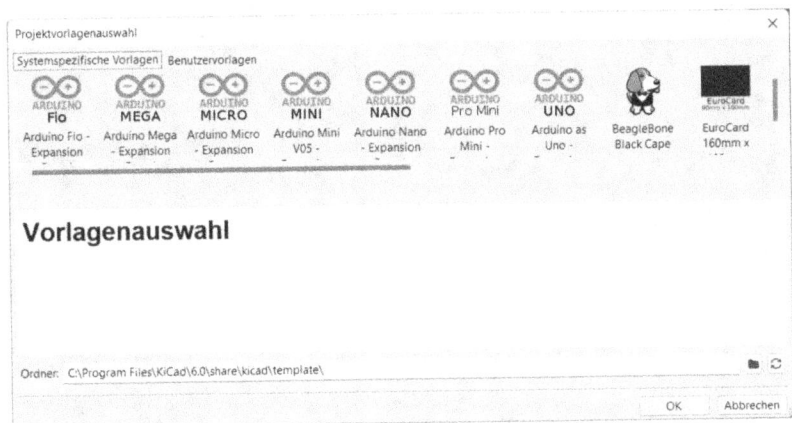

Fig. 12: Template

With the menu *File → New Project from Template* you can open existing project templates.

But often you want to use your own template or adapt an existing one to your own requirements. We have the folder for our own templates under the path settings (KICAD_USER_TEMPLATE_DIR). We can store our templates there. To do this, a project is simply created (see next chapter) and saved. This folder can now be placed in the directory for the user templates. But that's not a template yet! If we look into the templates folder, which is under KiCad in the program folder, we see that there is another folder called meta in the templates.

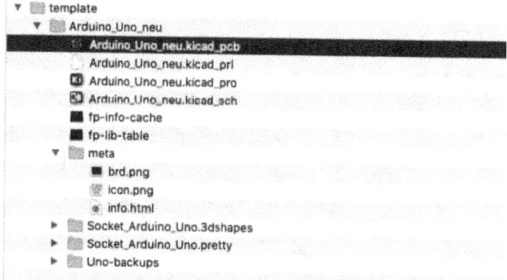

Fig. 13: Der Ordner *meta* im Verzeichnis des Templates

Simply copy a folder into the newly created directory. The info.html file is important. This describes the template. The <TITLE> tag and the text in the <BODY> should be adjusted. The icon.png and brd.png images are optional. This allows you to display the icon and insert a preview of the board. If you don't want to display the board, then you have to delete the <IMG> tag in info.html.

Chapter 3
Schematic Editor

3 The Schematic

3.1 Schematic Editor interface

When you create a new project (or a new one from a template), you initially have two files: one with the extension *.kicad_sch and one with *.kicad_pcb. From the icon you can already see that it is the circuit on the one hand and the circuit board on the other.

Let's look at the schematic here first.

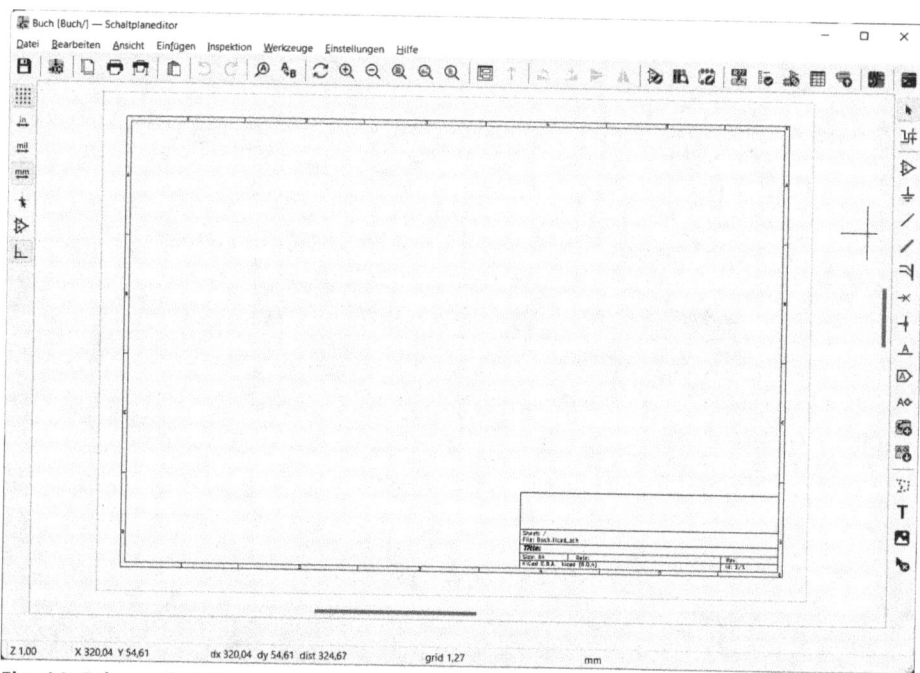

Fig. 14: Schematic Editor Interface

There are three bars with icons. If you move the mouse over the icons, an explanation will open. That's why I don't want to write down all the explanations again. They are usually easy to understand.

The left bar allows setting the units of measurement, the grid and showing hidden pins. The latter icon allows the display of pins that are actually not essential for the function (e.g. operating voltage and ground). For example, if there are four gates on a circuit (e.g. 7400), they share a common power supply. There VCC is on pin 14 and GND on pin 7. For the board, GND is automatically connected to ground and VCC to the voltage VCC. You don't have to specify it separately. There just needs to be a GND and VCC. More on that later.

The top bar contains what you have always known: save, print, back, forward. The third icon from the left 🗋 concerns the form.

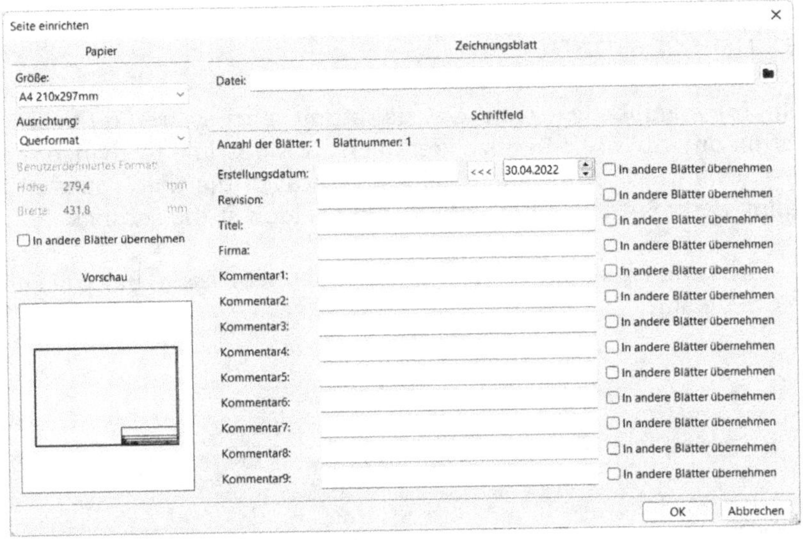

Fig. 15: Page settings

At the top left I can select the one that suits the project from the pre-made sheets. If I need my own, I can also create it with the *Drawing Sheet Editor* (see page 19). I can store my own drawing sheet in my folder system and call it up again later via *File* (at the top of the window). The remaining lines should be self-explanatory.

The icons at the top right are used for organization and interaction with the board editor. I can search, create, edit or even delete schematic symbols and footprints. Furthermore, the components are assigned reference values (i.e. they are numbered consecutively) and then the individual components are assigned the corresponding footprint. The latter is important because many components can have completely different designs. The so-called Electrical Rule Check (ERC) serves to check whether all components are correctly connected to one another. With BOM you can create a component list. But we prefer to do that with a plugin in the circuit board editor. The circuit board

Chapter 3: Schematic Editor

editor opens with the icon. We can always switch back and forth between the two views.

The right side houses the editing tools for the schematic. Important are the tools for marking, adding components, connections and buses as well as identifiers. I think that hierarchical schematics are not used, at least initially. So let's just ignore the icons.

3.2 Set up schematic

Here you will probably mostly leave the basic settings as they are. In the symbol unit notation one can use reference identifiers. It is possible to change the warning messages for ERC in the electrical rules. Most of the time you won't change anything here. But it can be useful to simply look at the settings.

Various line widths and types can be predefined under net classes. But you will mostly leave the default.

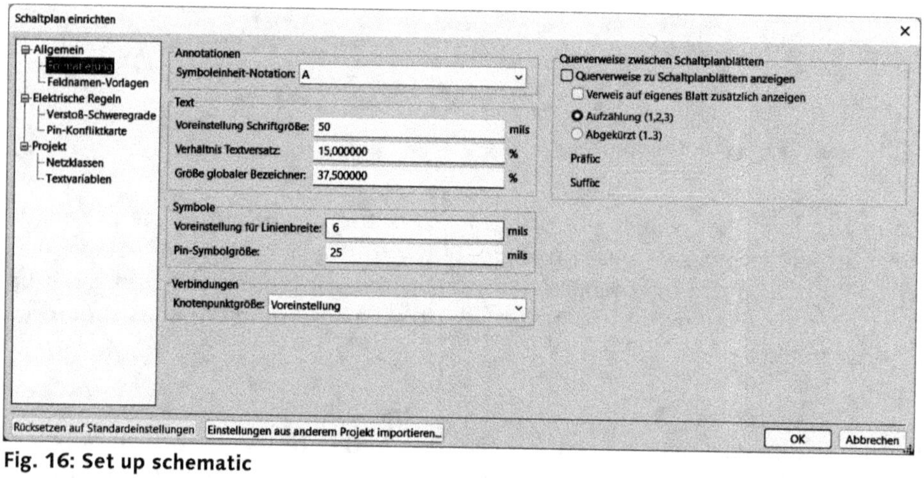

Fig. 16: Set up schematic

3.3 Drawing the schematic

To draw the components, we click on the OPV symbol on the far right ▷ or simply enter the letter A. A window for selecting symbols opens. The symbols are read from the symbol library. Since there are quite a few, it will take a while. I can use the search function to look for components. Some of them already exist with the type designation. As a rule, however, you will look for the type (e.g. npn or resistor). Even if you have set the user interface to German, you have to search with the English terms here. Often with several different terms. For many components there are circuit symbols according to both US and EU standards. If you find absolutely nothing, or the circuit drawing does not conform to the desired standard, you can use the symbol editor to change circuit symbols or create new ones. Just bring up the icon editor (it's in the top icon row), find the icon you want to change, double click and change. Either you change it forever or save it under a different name. You can also create new symbols in this way. But changing is faster...

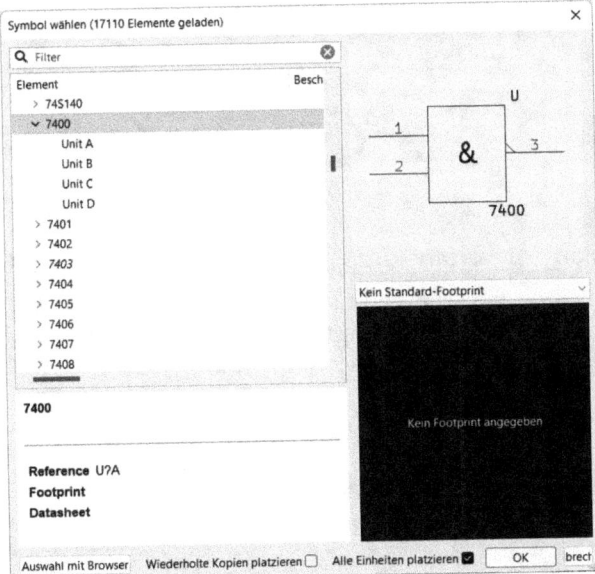

Fig. 17: Selection of circuit symbols

It can be useful to write down the names of frequently used symbols that you have finally found after a long search. This saves you searching time later. Already used symbols appear at the top of the list. With each click, the symbol window opens again (recognizable by the icon with the OPV). If you don't want to insert any more symbols, click on the arrow on the far right or simply press the ESC key. Right-clicking on the component opens a window that allows you to edit the location and properties.

Chapter 3: Schematic Editor

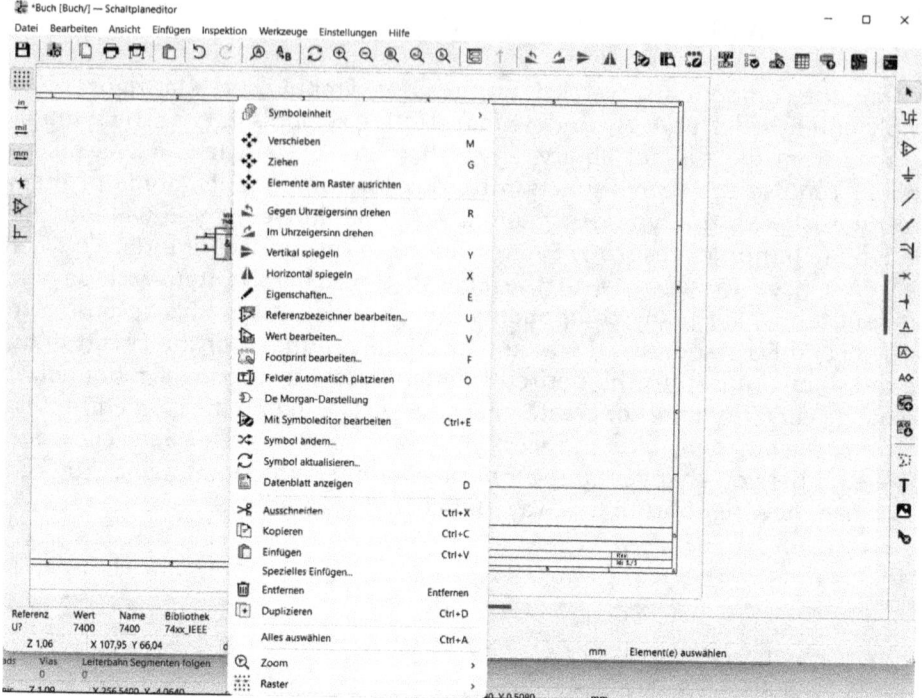

Fig. 18: Bearbeitung des Symbols

These keys would be particularly important (upper and lower case does not matter):

- M   Move

- R   Rotate Counterclockwise

- X   Mirror Horizontally

- E   Properties

Especially the properties (E) show everything you want to change. It is important that the cursor is positioned over the symbol.

In the reference we see the code letter and behind it a question mark. You could enter a serial number here. However, it is better to leave the question mark and leave the numbering to the program.

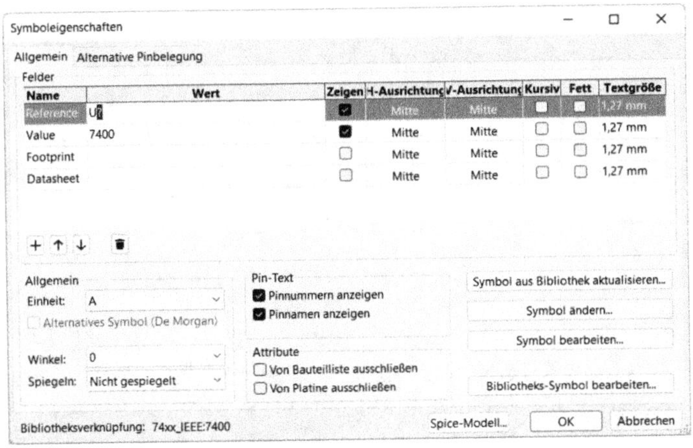

Fig. 19: Symbol properties

The *Value* of the component or its designation is entered under Value. First of all, the designation from the symbol list is in this field. Here it is 7400, for a resistance it could be R_Small for example. Then you simply write in the value that the component should have.

For some symbols, the footprint and possibly also the link to the data sheet is already entered. This saves the selection of the footprint afterwards. If nothing is entered, you could already select it here. But we are postponing that to a later date.

In the example, we see the letter A under *Unit* (found under *General* under the *Fields*). In our example component, there are four gates in one housing. They are numbered A, B, C and D. And this is the first gate. If you change the letter, the numbering of the connections also changes.

Code letters are used for classification. Unfortunately, this classification does not correspond to DIN EN 81346-2. In contrast to the old and withdrawn DIN 40719-2 from 1978, DIN EN 81346-2 describes the code letters according to the function instead of the type of component. If you want to label according to the standard, you can change the letter either here or in the symbol library.

In the following table Tab. 2 I have listed the information that is of interest to us. The standard also includes tasks that apply to mechanical objects.

Rotating and moving works not only for the symbol, but also for the *Reference* and the *Value*. You just have to move the cursor over the relevant element.

Once you have placed the symbols you want on the canvas, deselect the tool by pressing ESC or clicking the right arrow. If you want to duplicate an icon: right-click on the icon and then select Duplicate.

code letter	purpose or task	example
A	Two or more purposes or tasks	module
B	Conversion of an input variable into a signal intended for further processing	Sensor, Photocell, Microphone, Voltage Transformer, Measuring Transformer, Overload Relay
C	Storage of energy or information	Capacitor, Coil, Battery, RAM, EPROM
E	Delivery of radiation or thermal energy	Incandescent lamp, UV radiator
F	Direct (automatic) protection of a power or signal flow	Fuse, Residual Current operated Circuit-Breaker
G	initiating a flow of energy; Generate signals that serve as a source of information or reference	Generator, solar cell, signal generator, pump, blower
K	Processing of signals or information	Relays, transistors, binary elements, controllers, input/output modules, optocouplers
M	Provision of mechanical energy for drive purposes	electric motor, electromagnet
P	presentation of information	Indicator light, multifunction meter, display, horn
Q	Controlled switching or varying of a power or signal flow	Circuit breaker, contactor, thyristor, earth electrode
R	Limiting or stabilizing the flow of energy or material	Resistor, choke, diode, filter
S	Conversion of a manual operation into a signal intended for further processing	Switch, keyboard, button
T	Conversion of energy or signals while retaining the type of energy or the information content	Transformer, DC/DC converter, frequency converter, rectifier, amplifier, antenna
U	Holding objects in a defined position	Mounting plate, subrack, printed circuit board
W	Conducting or carrying power or signals	Data bus, control cable, measuring cable, fiber optic cable
X	connecting objects	Terminal, socket, connector, connecting element, signal distributor

Tab. 2: Kennbuchstaben nach DIN EN 81346-2

The individual connections must now be connected. This is done either with the tool *Add a Wire [W]* ∕ or you *Add a Bus* ∕. I'll limit myself to the first option here. The bus is basically the same.

Chapter 3: Schematic Editor   31

There are small circles on the connectors on the symbols. These are the points where the ladder docks. Here we add the connection. The connection points must be connected to each other. For certain applications it may prove necessary to leave a line open. Then simply click twice and the open end is marked with a small square.

It is important to ensure that the symbols also lie on the grid. Otherwise the connecting line will not "dock". As can be seen in Fig. 20, I added net identifiers (*Label*) [*L*] (OUT and SIGNAL). These are useful when connections are to be made over long distances and to multiple locations in the circuit. Nets with the same name are always connected to each other. In the example, pins 2, 6, 12 and 13 as well as 1, 4, 5 and 8 are connected to each other, even if the connections themselves are not drawn. The icon of the network identifier is simply clicked (or typed an *L*). The name of the network is entered in the window that opens. After OK, the network designation hangs on the cursor. The small square is then simply clicked on a connection line or the open end of the connection line and the connection now has the net designation. This way you can create nice and clear circuit diagrams.

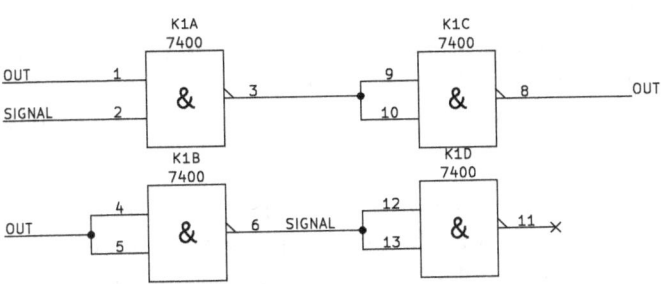

Fig. 20: Connections between components

A small cross can be seen on pin 11. This is the *Add a no-connection flag [Q]*. Each terminal of a component must be connected to another. If there are connectors that are not used (i.e., "hanging in the air"), which is often the case with circuits, they must be so labeled. Otherwise you will get an error message during the ERC check.

The 7400 circuit used in the example also requires an operating voltage. It cannot be seen here. For the following screenshot (Fig. 21) I switched on the display of the hidden pins.

It can be seen in gray in the background that pin 14 is labeled VCC and pin 7 is labeled GND. These connections are otherwise not visible in the circuit. To add the operating voltage and ground there must be a net with (in this case)

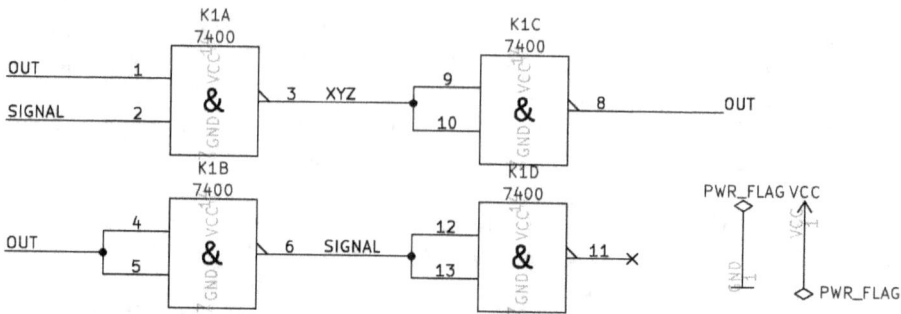

Fig. 21: power connections

GND and VCC. If I envisaged a power supply, there will be something like this. But I don't have anything like that here yet. I just add the GND and VCC symbol from the *power* library. The PWR_FLAG is added to show that these are operating voltages. This flag does not appear later on the board. At the ERC check, it only states that it is power. When determining the network, you only have to make sure that the designation of the network of the operating voltage matches that of the circuit. (here VCC).

We have now made the electrical connections. Let's now turn to mechanical parts. These are holes that are required to attach components or assemblies or small heat sinks that are to be attached and of course also take up space. There is a *Mechanical* item under the symbols.

Once the circuit has been drawn, the references and footprints must be assigned and a check made to ensure that no systematic errors have crept in. Unfortunately, errors in reasoning in the circuit design cannot be found.

For the further explanation we now take the following circuit.

By clicking the Reference Identifier icon all components that have a question mark after the code letter are assigned a consecutive number.

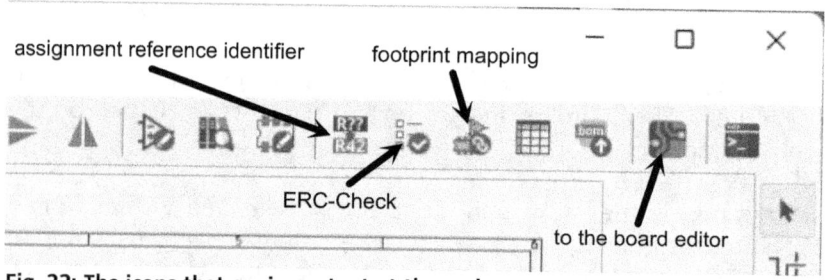

Fig. 22: The icons that are important at the end

Chapter 3: Schematic Editor

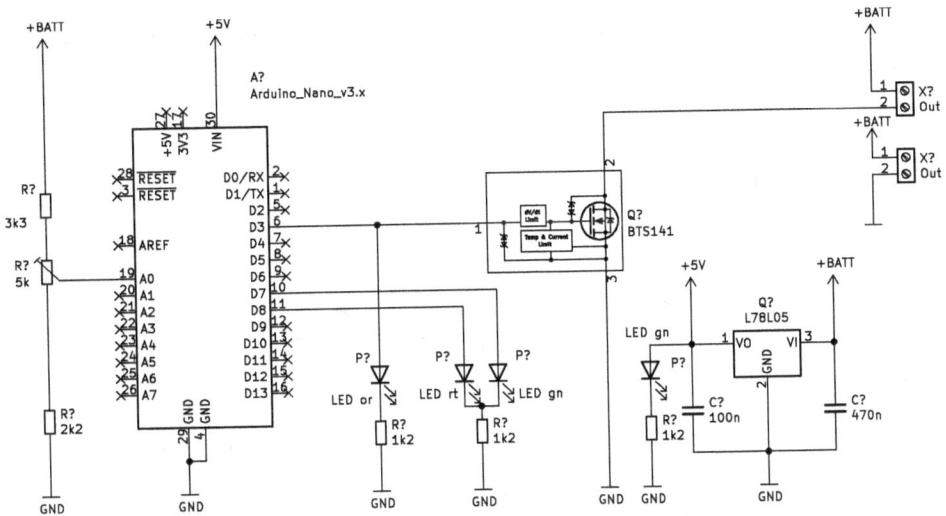

Fig. 23: Schematic - still without assignment of the reference designator

The order can be set, but the default is probably sufficient. If you have already referenced components, they will be skipped. The whole thing now looks like this:

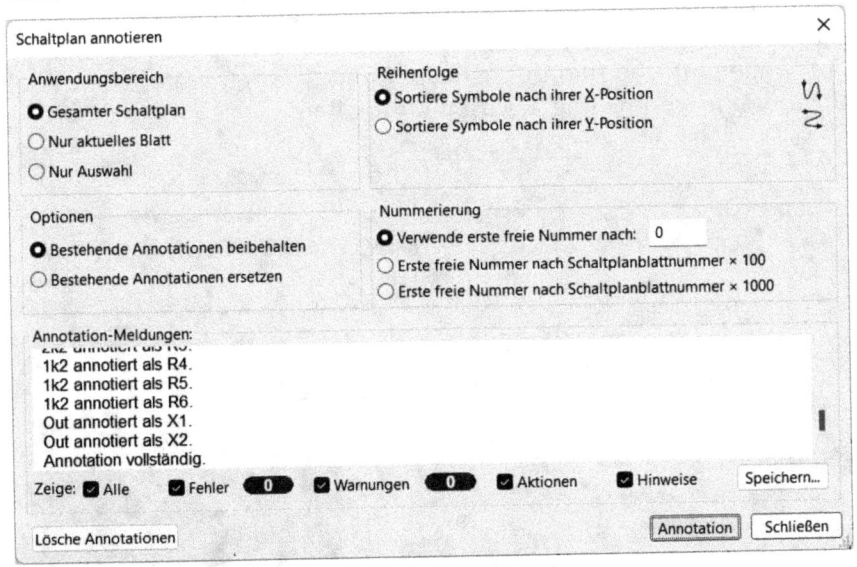

Fig. 24: Fill in schematic symbol reference designators

All components are now numbered (Fig. 25) and each of them still needs a footprint to be assigned (Fig. 26). Here it is also determined in which connection grid e.g. wired components are used. However, you can change this later if necessary. However, this should always happen in the circuit so that the circuit and the board are consistent with each other.

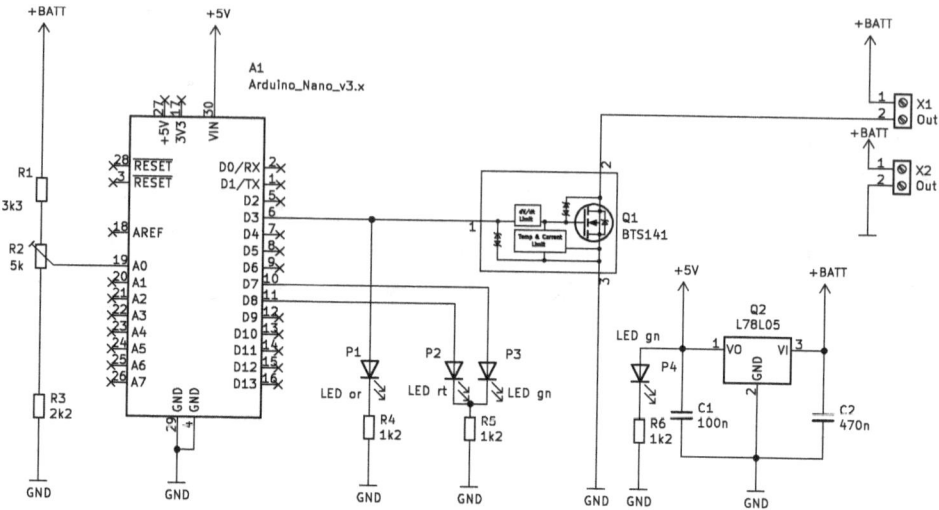

Fig. 25: The referenced schematic

You can view the selected footprint by clicking the right mouse button. Here in the picture the trimmer. If you don't know the exact name, you have to search for a while until you find the right footprint. It can therefore be useful to note down the footprints that are used more often.

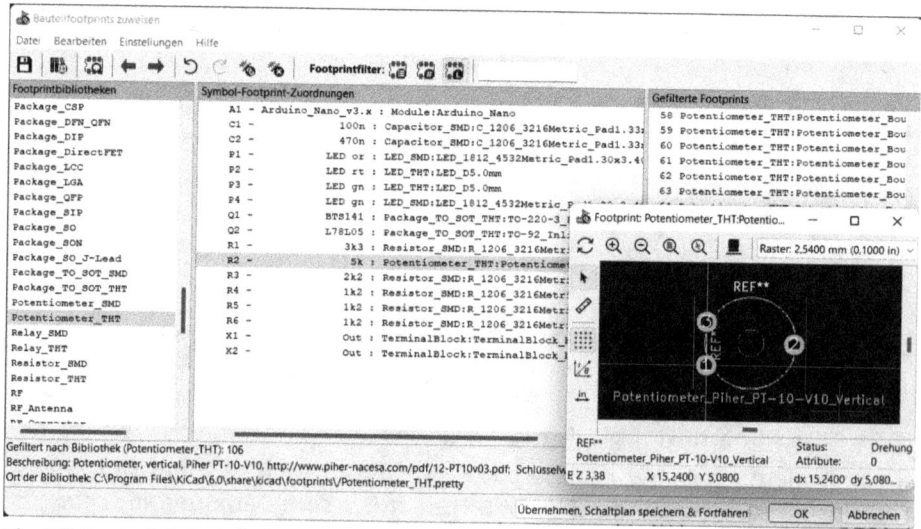

Fig. 26: Footprint-Zuweisung

If all components are assigned the appropriate footprint, you should do the ERC check ✓.

But don't forget to save the footprints first.

In our example, two errors are now displayed. Q2 expects an input voltage

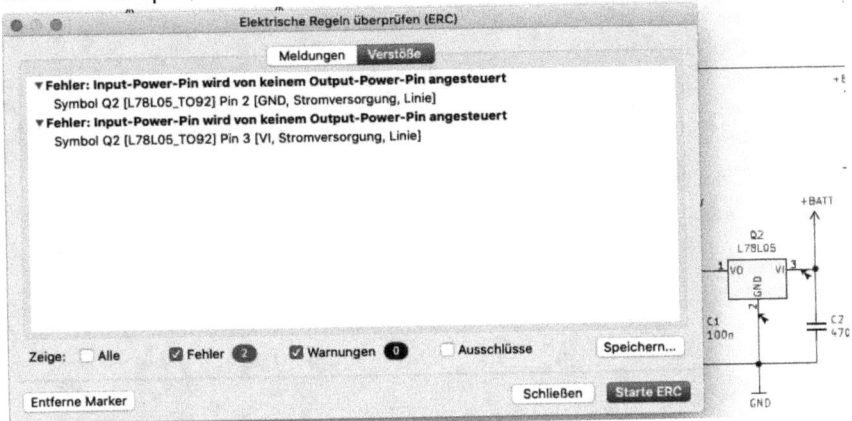

Fig. 27: ERC check with errors

and a ground. The fault location is also indicated by arrows (markers). Here at Q2.

We know that +BATT is the voltage source and X2 is the connection to it. In fact, we could just ignore it. But it is better if we eliminate the source of the error and mark GND and +BATT as power sources:

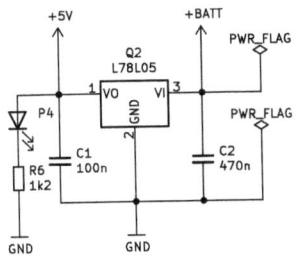

Fig. 28: Added power flags

A new check should no longer show any error messages.

Which error messages and warnings are displayed during the ERC check can be specified in the settings. I would leave the default settings as they are. The individual symbols always specify what inputs, outputs or power supply connections are and which connections should not be checked.

You could change it in the symbol library. That also makes sense for self-modified symbols for components that are not in the library. But otherwise you should look for the error and fix it as above.

Chapter 4
PCB Editor

4 PCB Editor

4.1 PCB Editor interface

The board editor is accessed via the board editor icon (see Fig. 22). A new window opens, which also has a drawing sheet again (this time with a dark background) and completely different icons.

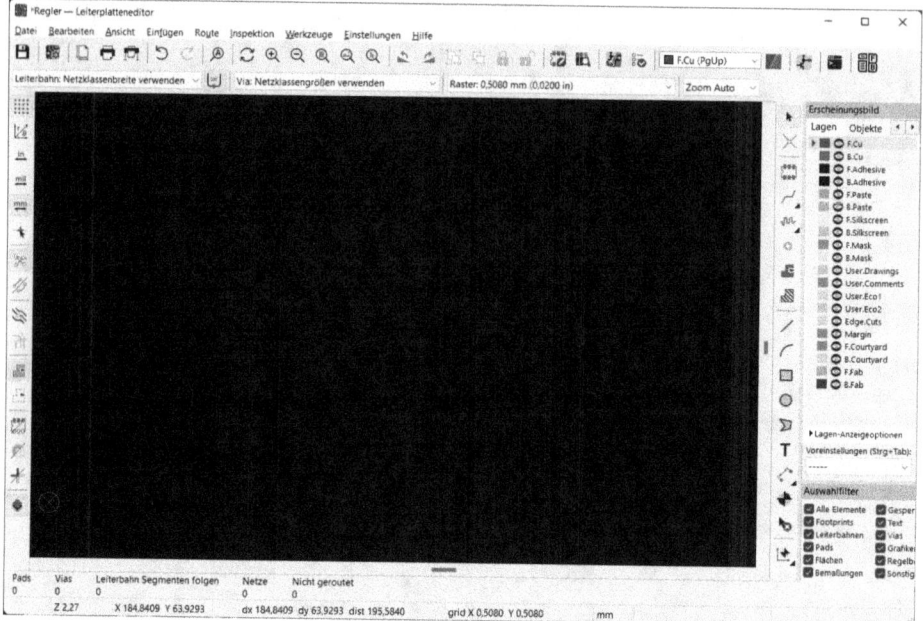

Fig. 29: Oberfläche des Platineneditors

On the left side you can set various settings for the view:

- Units

- Grid

- Representation of air lines, traces, pins, areas

As always, hovering over the icon will show a description. Actually, everything is self-explanatory, which is why I refrain from further explanations.

The upper side is divided in two. At the top are icons. In addition to the usual ones (save, print, magnifying glass) you can fix elements with the lock. But the icons next to it are more interesting. In addition to those for editing footprints, the icon for accepting changes to the circuit diagram is important. Anyone who has worked with KiCad version 5 (or earlier) will remember that a network map had to be updated each time. That's gone now. The changes in the circuit can be applied directly.

Next to it is the Design Rules Check (DRC) icon. Here it is checked whether the specified distances, conductor sizes, labels, etc. are observed. Errors are displayed with arrows and text similar to the ERC check.

The triangle on the scroll bar next to it shows the currently active level. I'll get to the levels in a moment. The following icon defines the front and back. For double-sided boards, this icon is actually less important. You just leave everything as it is.

With the icon that represents a circuit diagram, we come back to the circuit diagram editor. So we can easily switch back and forth between the two. This allows quick changes to be made in the circuit diagram or to the footprint assignments (e.g. changing the grid width for wired components). But after that keep pressing the icon for changes to the schematic (or F8).

I think that, at least initially, nobody will work with Python scripts. Therefore we skip the following icon. We added the last icon at the very beginning with the *Plugin and Content Manager*. Once the board is designed, an interactive bill of materials can be created here. This is displayed in a browser. Hovering over a component name with the mouse will show where the component is located on the board. Actually quite practical.

Below the icons are scroll bars for setting line widths, vias (these are the plated-through holes) and the grid. The grid should be an integer divisor of the connection grid of the components. Don't choose too roughly! If I want to route a conductor between two pins of a circuit, the grid has to be quite fine.

The menu on the right is divided into two again. On the one hand there are different icons for editing and next to them the layers on which we work. The icons represent an essential selection. All options can be selected under Insert, Route and Inspection of the upper toolbar. The icons shown on the right are what you actually need all the time. With the icons, which have a small triangle at the bottom right, you can set further options with the right mouse button.

Let's look at the most important ones first. The arrow is at the top again ⬉ for selecting elements, which can always be reached with ESC. Individual elements can be selected. Then they get lighter. They can be moved with M, rotated with R, etc. Similar to the symbols in the schematic editor. Right-clicking will reveal all functions, including keyboard shortcuts.

If the desktop is still empty, which is probably the case at this point, not much is displayed when you press the right mouse button. But that changes when elements are placed.

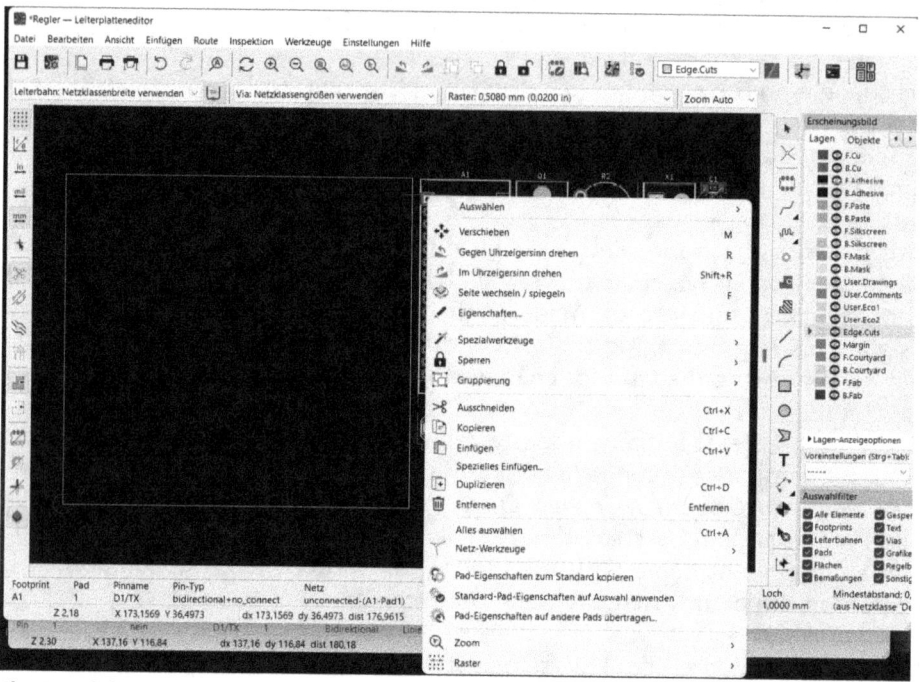

Fig. 30: Right mouse button on an element

The next interesting icon is *Add a Footprint [A]* . The footprints are placed with the components that we later take from the circuit diagram. But we can later use this icon to create logos etc. created with the image converter. take over and bring to the board. I'll come back to that.

One of the most important icons here is *Route tracks [X]* . The right triangle below allows you to set the mode. The right mouse button shows options how to handle DRC violations:

- Router Highlight Mode
  This shows where there are collisions. I can still run the conductor path through there.

- Router Shove Mode
  Existing traces and vias are moved.

- Router Walkaround Mode
  When routing traces, an attempt is made to find a way to circumvent the DRC violation. This is the default setting and should be left as it is.

Adjust the *Tune length of a single track [7]* icon makes it possible to create defined conductor lengths. If it is too short, it will be lengthened with wavy lines. This function is not so interesting for normal electronic circuits. It's different when you're working with microwaves (there are more options under *Place → Add Microwave Shape*).

Add free-standing vias [Ctrl + Shift + V] with a via can be added without traces. This can be used if, for example, you have large ground planes on both sides and want to connect them to each other. We create vias on conductor tracks differently (will come when we deal with the routes).

It may be that there should be areas on the board that should be free of vias, pads and conductors or copper areas. With you can define restricted areas. This should be done early in the board design. Then these areas are taken into account when routing.

Use *Add filled zone [Ctrl + Shift + Z]* to fill empty spaces. In the dialog you determine whether they should be connected to a network (e.g. GND). The areas are then filled with *Edit → Fill All Zones [B]*. The view can be switched on and off with the icon on the far left.

This can be undone with [Ctrl + B].

The following five icons are used to draw lines and bodies. We need them for labels and borders. After that comes the annotation tool. With the next, dimensions can be made and orientation points can be set.

The delete tool can be used to delete elements. This also works if you select it and press the delete key. The tool is useful if you want to remove several elements one after the other.

The *point of origin for drill files and component placement files* is placed on the lower left corner of the circuit board outline.

To the right of the icons is the *Appearance* field. What we need above all here are the layers. When the circuit board is designed, it is essential to manufacture what is needed at which manufacturing step. Even if we make the board ourselves, we need to know what is the top and what is the bottom. Information about the components is taken from the circuit diagram (designation, values, outlines, etc.). When I create the slides for the exposure for myself, of course I only want the conductor tracks on it and not the rest. Therefore, the individual information is placed on different layers. Anyone who has worked with design or image processing programs already knows this system.

The individual levels are marked with colors and have a name. There is an "eye" between the two. If you click on it, you can turn the display on or off. Many designations are preceded by an F or a B. The F stands for front, the B for back. Conductors, components and labels can be attached to both sides of double-sided printed circuit boards. If you want to use more than two layers, additional prefixes are added for the copper layers (e.g. in1, in2).

The current level is indicated by a small triangle in front of it. It is also displayed in the top page in the scroll bar. I can select it there or I can just click on the layer I want to edit.

So that the right thing is done at the right level, I have listed in the following table Tab 3 which level means what.

If we expose and etch the boards ourselves, we only need to print out the F.Cu and B.Cu. We simply set that in the print menu. We need the other layers when we create the Gerber files for PCB service providers. I'll come back to that later.

The Objects and Networks tabs can be used to selectively show or hide individual elements.

Layer	Meaning	Remark
F.Cu	copper surface above or below	
B.Cu		
F.Adhesive	glue for SMD	we usually won't need it
B.Adhesive		
F.Paste	area for solder paste	is needed if you have a mask for the solder paste and then solder SMD with hot air
B.Paste		
F.Silkscreen	annotation layer	if you want your own inscriptions to appear on the circuit board later, you write them on this layer
B.Silkscreen		
F.Mask	soldermask	Service providers print solder resist masks that only expose the soldering pads. This prevents solder bridges.
B.Mask		
Edge.Cuts	outer edges of the board	Here we set the dimensions of the board. For many service providers, it does not have to be rectangular, but can also have other shapes.
F.Courtyard	physical location of the components on the PCB	it is a rectangular border
B.Courtyard		
F.Fab	fabrication level	Mainly used for documentation. Here are the reference designation and the value of the component again. Don't confuse it with the silkscreen - you want the silkscreen as an imprint, but usually not fab.
B.Fab		
Margin	we don't use it	
User...	we don't use it	

Tab. 3: Meaning of the layers

4.2 Board Setup

The basic configuration can be accessed via *File* → *Board Setup* or the icon in the upper icon bar (second from the left). You can simply take over many values. However, I recommend the following changes to start with:

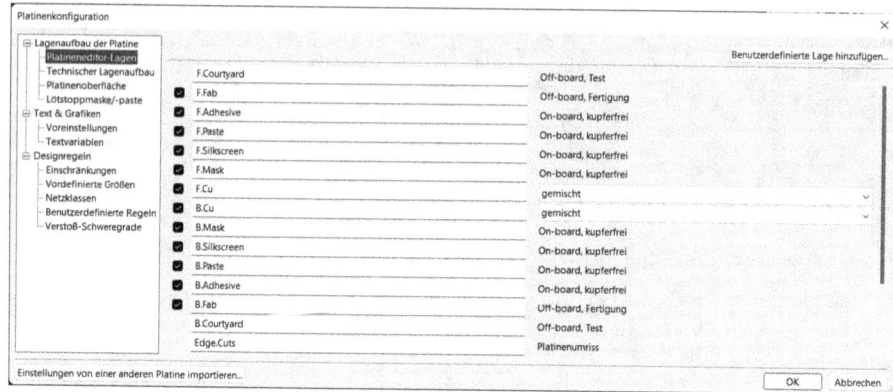

Fig. 31: Board Stackup: Board Editor Layers

For the two copper layers we set *mixed*. With more than two layers, it makes sense to use inner layers for power and ground and outer layers for signals only. With two layers, both signals and operating voltages can be found on the two copper layers.

You can also deselect levels that you don't need here. Eligible would be the levels beginning with *User*. You should just leave the others alone. We will hardly need F.Fab and B.Fab later, but now they help us to find the right components.

Let's take a look at the following menu items of the board configuration. Hardly anything can be changed here. Unless you have very special circuit board materials or different copper strengths than normal.

With the *Physical Stackup*, we determine how many layers we use. It can be seen that single-layer circuit boards are not intended at all. But that is not a problem: it is then simply routed on the B.Cu level. FR4 is entered as the standard board material. This material is the most used. But you can also change it. But unless we're doing top-to-bottom line or pad capacitance calculations, the material isn't really that important. We read through the other following settings and leave them as they are for now.

When setting up the schematic, we left the default for net classes. Here we leave it at this value.

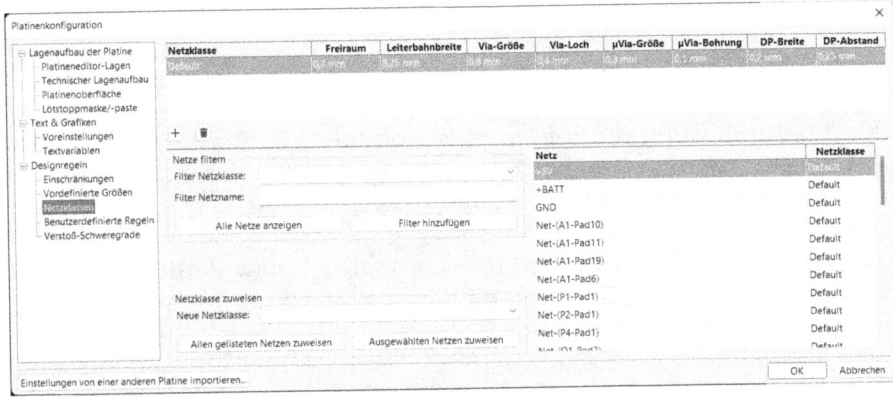

Fig. 32: Design Rules: Net Classes

If we don't specify anything else later for the conductor widths and vias, these values will be used. The via hole diameter of 0.4mm is also chosen by service providers. You can change it if, for example, you want to use through-hole rivets (from Bungard, for example) on self-made boards or if you need larger ones for load reasons.

However, we make changes to *Pre-defined Sizes*. Here we create at least a few additional conductor widths. The default values of the net classes are retained.

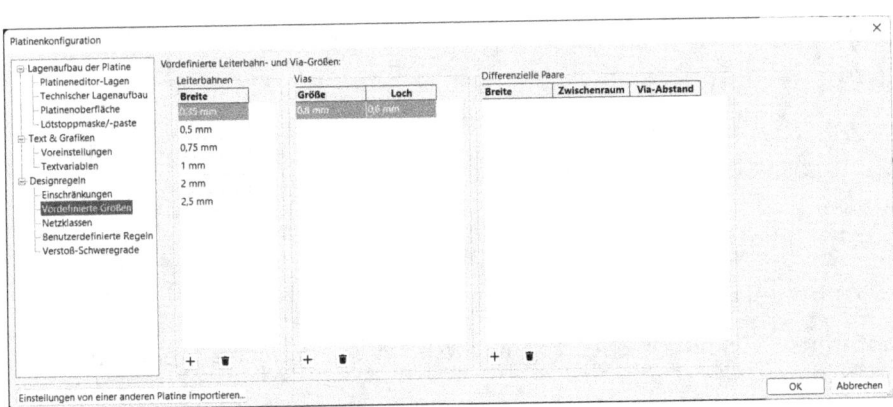

Fig. 33: Design Rules: Pre-defined Sizes

Which widths we add depends on the later use. If we didn't take a specific width into account - no problem: everything can be changed or added later.

4.3 Routing

Let's start with the development of the circuit board.

On the empty black drawing sheet we first determine the dimensions or outlines of the future circuit board. To do this, we activate the Edge.Cuts layer with a mouse click. With the line, rectangle or polygon tool (circle will probably be less interesting) we define the outer edges. The point of origin for the drilling files can then also be placed on the lower left corner.

Then we get the values generated by the schematic editor with the *Update PCB with changes made to schematic* icon [F8].

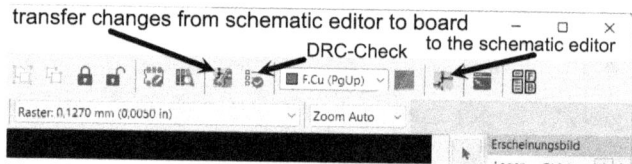

Fig. 34: Icons top

The window that opens now appears every time we make an update from the schematic. At the top you can specify what should happen with the changes. We click the *Update PCB* button.

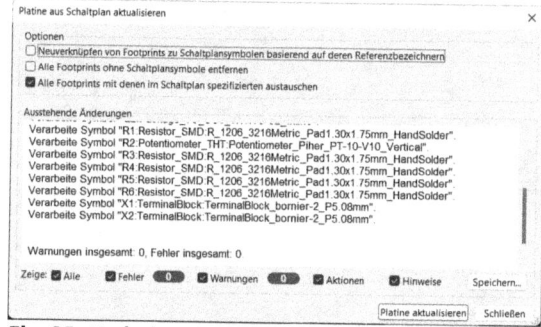

Fig. 35: Updating the schematic

All footprints are now attached to the cursor. We first place all footprints next to the board outline (Fig. 36).

Footprints of SMD components are now initially on the upper side (F.Cu) (can be recognized by the red color - if nothing has been changed). When routing, we always look at the board from above - no matter what level we are working on.

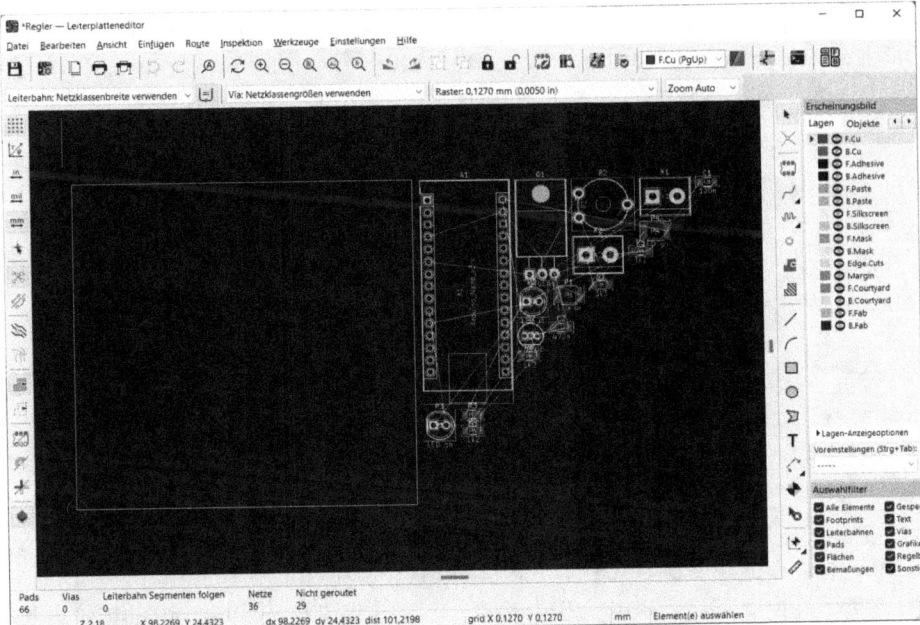

Fig. 36: Component footprints and airwires next to the board outline

Further we see that all the pins are connected with thin lines according to the connections in the schematic. These are the so-called "airwires". These remain until the pins of the components are actually connected by conductor tracks. This allows you to see if any connections are still missing. The airwires are attached to the pins and move when we move or rotate the components.

Before we start with the placement, let's take a look at the grid. The setting for this is located directly above the workspace. After all, we want the pins and conductors to really meet, and maybe a conductor should lead between two IC pins. So let's look at which component has the smallest distance between the pins. With an IC in a DIP package it is 2.54 mm (0.1 in), with an SMD resistor 0805 (you can hardly make it smaller with a soldering iron and hand soldering, I prefer 1206 as a design) the distance between two soldering surfaces is 0.8 mm. In order to run a conductor there, the grid should be 0.254 mm (= 10 mil) or less. Click on the component to move it. It is important to ensure that the entire component is activated and not just a part of it. You can tell by the fact that it gets brighter. With the M key and the mouse button pressed, we can now place the components on the circuit board. The criteria explained in Chapter 1 must be taken into account.

The building elements are to be moved and turned in such a way that there are as few crossings of the airwires as possible. Intersections can always cause problems since we are locked into the levels above and below. With two-sided boards you can switch to the other side. With one-sided one is forced to use wire bridges if necessary.

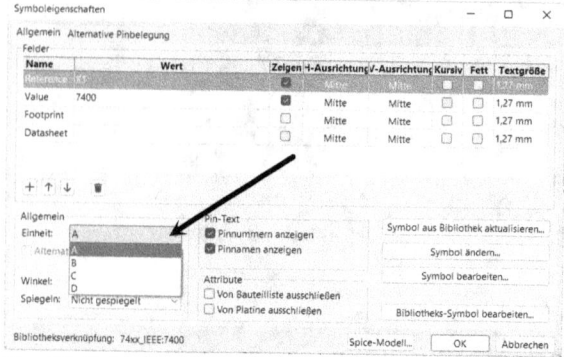

Fig. 37: Gate-Swapping

To avoid crossings, we try to simplify the layout with pin and gate swaps. To do this, however, we have to switch back to the circuit diagram editor. This is very easy: at the top of the icon bar we have the circuit diagram editor icon (see Fig. 34). Just click on the icon and we are back at the schematic editor.

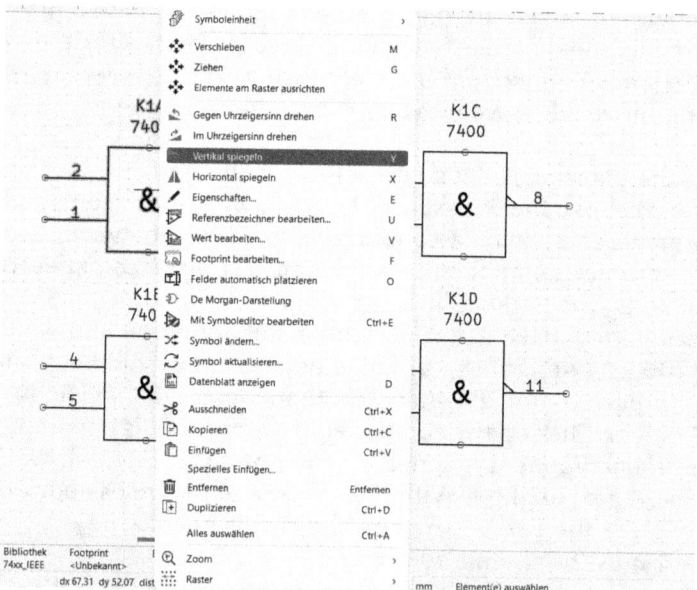

Fig. 38: Mirroring the pins

Chapter 4: PCB Editor

Gateswapping is done when there are multiple devices in one package (e.g. 7400 has four gates). To do this, place the cursor on the gate and call up the properties (press the E key).

The individual gates are marked with letters (e.g. K1A, K1B etc.). If A is to be swapped with B, K1A is changed to B and K1B to A. The gates are now swapped.

Pin swapping can get a bit more complicated. You can try swapping the pins with mirror.

As in the example with two pins, it works without any problems. If it's not that easy, there's nothing left but to delete connections and reconnect.

The circuit is thus changed and saved. Clicking on the icon at the top right brings us back to the board editor. Please do not click on the circuit board in the view with the project files. Otherwise it can happen that we have several views open.

In the board editor we have to accept the changes. We either press F8 or use the mouse to click the Transfer changes to the schematic to the board icon

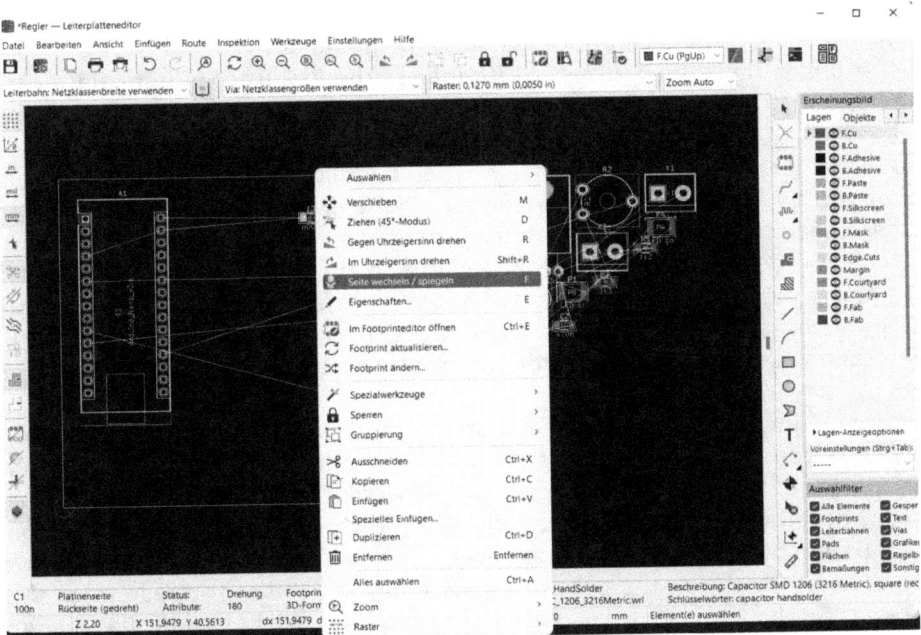

Fig. 39: Bring SMD components to the other side

(top left next to DRC-Check). The query appears again (Fig. 35), which we confirm.

When we've added new building elements, they appear on the side. With *Move [M]* and *Rotate [R]* we move the components as we deem appropriate. Always make sure that the whole component is selected and not just parts of it or just the label!

Especially SMD components can be placed on both sides. By default, they are displayed on the top side. If you want them to be placed on the bottom one: right click and select *Change Side/Flip* (or F key) (Fig. 39).

Since the part is now on the other side, it is shown in the color of B.Cu and the label is mirrored. I think the formerly common designation of assembly and conductor side is inappropriate. SMD components in particular can be mounted above and below, depending on requirements.

Once the components are placed, routing can begin. We will not find an auto router here. There are different opinions about autorouters anyway. A lot of users don't like it. So we route by hand...

First we mark the layer on which we want to start routing. It will mostly be the lower level (B.Cu). With Lay traces [X] we look for the first pin and look for the way to the target pin. Before doing so, you should set the width of the conductor under *Track: use netclass width* (above the workspace, immediately to the left).

You either start with critical points whose conductor paths must be adhered to, or you take the points that are already quite clear and easy to connect. If buffer capacitors are provided at the operating voltage connections of ICs, they should be arranged as close as possible to the operating voltage connection and ground, otherwise they will not serve their purpose. When routing, the program takes into account the distances specified in the configuration. If they cannot be met, the conductor will not be placed.

If you can't avoid crossings or they're on the other side of the board (especially SMD components), you have to get from one copper surface to the other. For this purpose, component connections of wired (TNT) components can be used. You move up to the pin and change the level. Then you can move on. Sometimes you just have to "jump" over a conductor path. This is where vias comes in handy. Move the path to where you want a via to appear, press the V key, click and the via will be created and the level will automatically change.

The size of the via depends on the settings that you have defined for it and set under Vias.

Just like the conductor widths, you can also change the values of the via later using the properties (key *E*). If you click on the track, the straight piece you hit will be activated and you can change it. If the entire trace is to be activated, enter the letter *U* – or right-click → *Select* → *Select/Expand Connection* or select all traces of a net.

In the course of routing you can get to the point where you can't get any further and have to delete traces that have already been routed in order to look for other paths. You just activate it and press the delete button. You can also use the delete tool in the right icon bar (at the bottom). If nothing works and you want to start over, global removal can be helpful (*Edit→Global Deletions*).

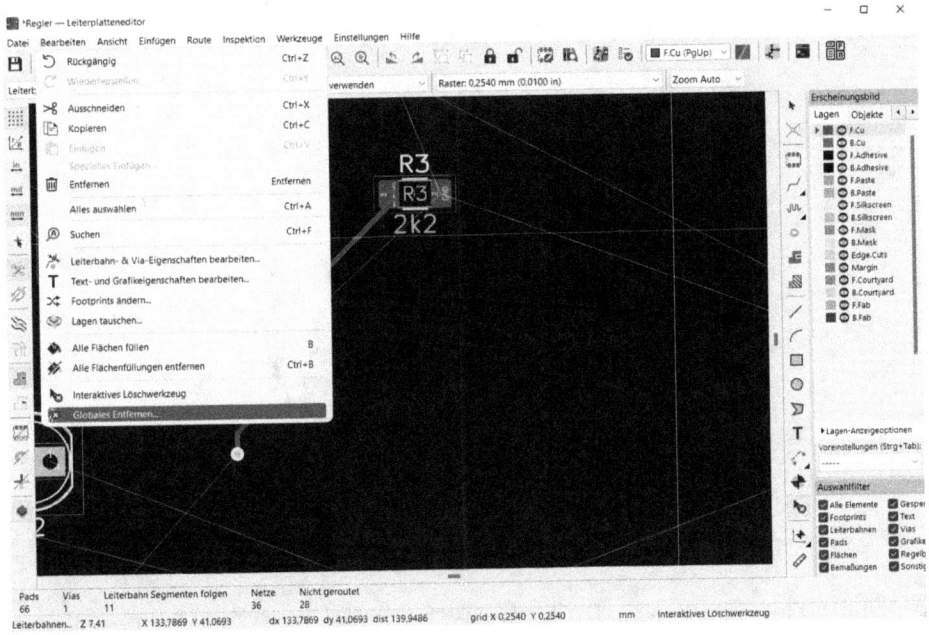

Fig. 40: Global Deletions

In the window that opens, select what you want to remove. After a security query, the action is carried out (Fig. 41).

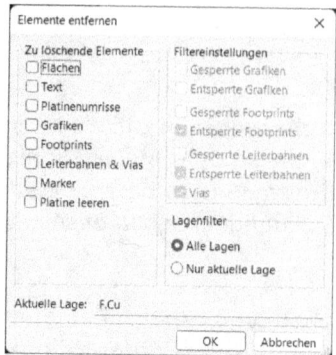

Fig. 41: Options Global Deletions

We have now made the electrical connections. Let's now turn to mechanical parts. We have provided them as a component in the circuit and provided them with values (here in the example a mounting hole for M 3 screws). If you activate it and go to the properties, you can still change the type and values.

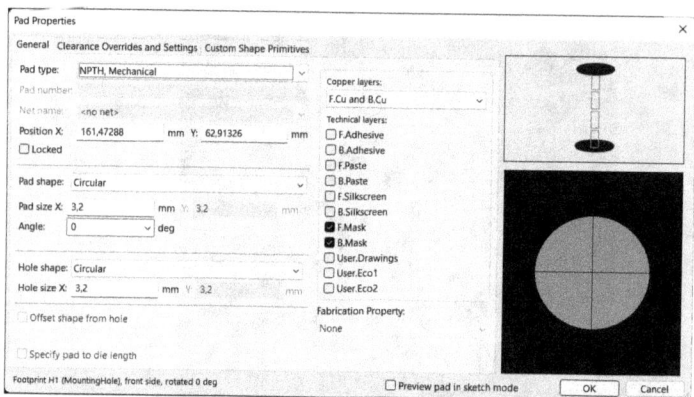

Fig. 42: Mechanical component - here a mounting hole

Next we'll add captions.

We will not want to use the levels F.Fab and B.Fab. The reference designations of the components (R1, R2, ...) are already on the F.Silkscreen or B.Silkscreen levels (depending on which side the component is on). In order for the labels to be printed later by a service provider, they have to be on the silkscreen layers. As you have already noticed, I always assume service providers. For a long time I always made the circuit boards myself. But if you search long enough and choose the right service provider, you can have the circuit boards manufactured very cheaply and in good quality. Under [3] I have noted a website in the bibliography that can help with the search. Of course, if I etch the circuit board myself, I don't print it. Then the inscriptions should consist of copper surfaces. Here you just have to be careful that they don't cause bridges.

In order to save etchant and/or to achieve a shield, you can fill areas that are not covered with conductor tracks with copper. This is then expediently connected to ground potential.

The tool Add a filled zone ![icon] I had already mentioned. If you select it and click on the first corner of the future surface, you will first be asked which surface you want to cover with which mesh and what the surface should look like. You can fill them as a grid or full.

Other parameters should actually be self-explanatory. Most of the time they will be left as they are.

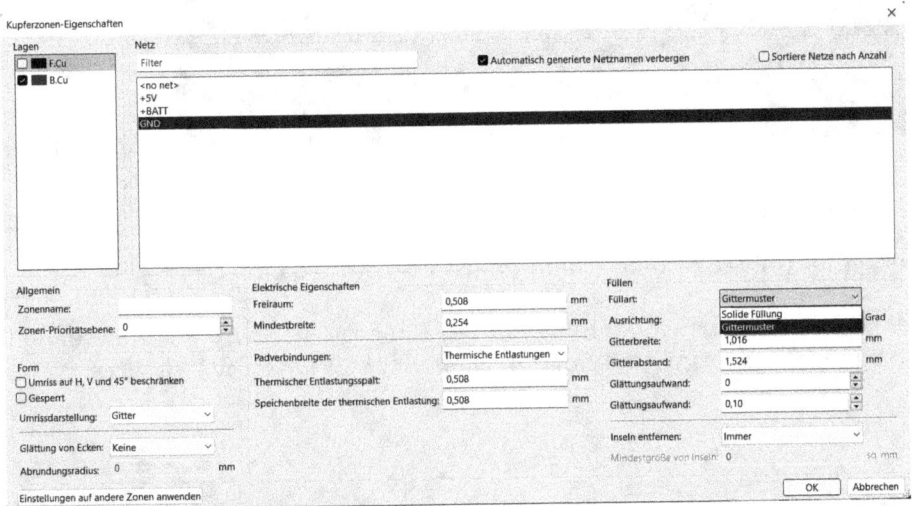

Fig. 43: Cooper Zone Properties

When drawing, make sure that you don't take the exact edge, but a little further inwards. Also make sure that the line is closed (ideally zoom in). If GND is chosen as the net, all ground planes will be connected together. Heat traps are also applied around the soldering points.

Chapter 4: PCB Editor

In the example, I created a solid page and a grid page.

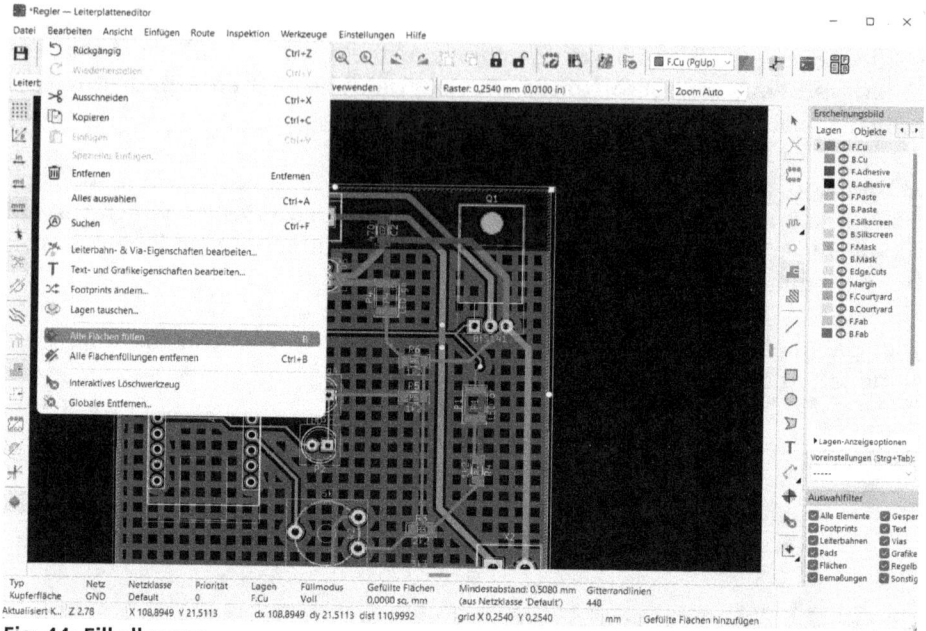

Fig. 44: Fill all zones

In order for the areas to be filled, it must be instructed (*Edit → Fill All Zones*).

Then you can see the whole thing in three dimensions. There are three-dimensional models for many (but not all) components (View → 3D Viewer).

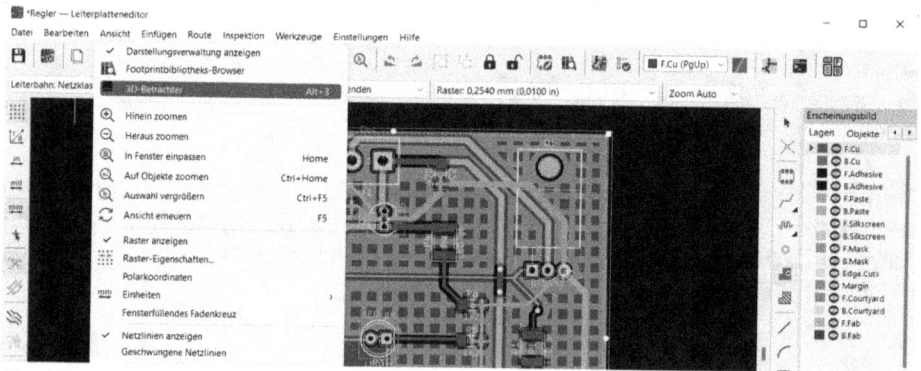

Fig. 45: 3D-Viewer

Chapter 4: PCB Editor   55

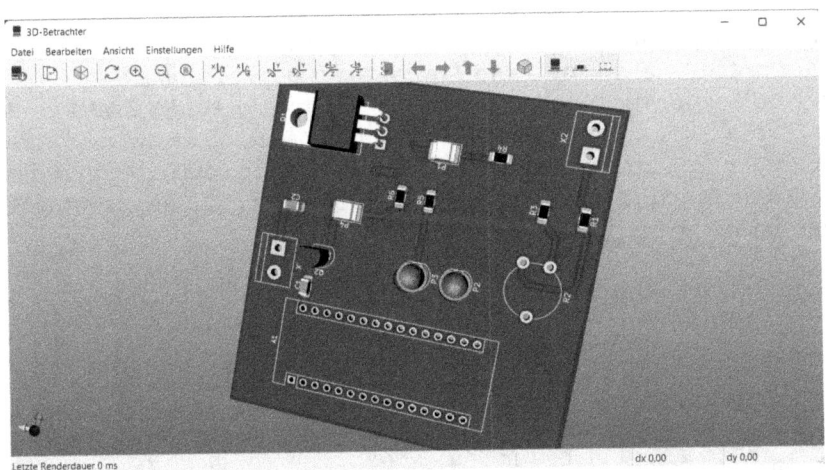

Fig. 46: 3D

If you expose and etch the board yourself, you only print out the copper areas (F.Cu or B.Cu) individually (or save them as a PDF in order to then combine them with a graphics program).

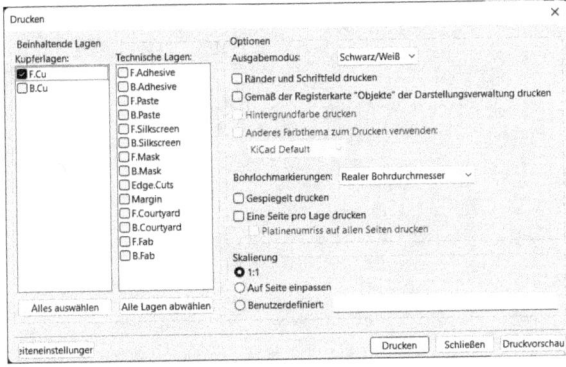

Fig. 47: Print menu

If you prepare the templates for exposure, make sure that the side of the foil that contains the printing ink comes onto the photoresist-coated circuit board. This prevents under-radiation. In this case, the layout may have to be mirrored when printing.

Hardly anyone in the hobby sector will have a real imagesetter. An inkjet printer can be used to print on transparent film. The resolution and density should be as high as possible.

I don't have an inkjet printer, I have a laser printer. The results on transparent film were not exactly convincing. *Films for print master production* were more suitable (try looking for them on the internet, in Germany: AVERY Zweckform No. 3491). These films are not transparent, but transparent. However, more transparent than normal tracing paper. The printout is then sprayed with toner compactor. You can get it from electronic mail order companies. The toner compressor makes the black really strong.

Maybe a hint about logos etc.:

With the image converter, an image is loaded and saved as a footprint and a front silkscreen in a folder.

This folder is added as a library under *Preferences* → *Manage Footprint Libraries*.

Add with footprint ⌗ the logo (or what you have saved there as an image) can be added to the circuit board. You can find this under the footprints under the alias of the library. You then have to call up the properties (*E* key) and uncheck the Reference designator checkbox.

Chapter 5
Files for board manufacturer

5 Fabrication Outputs

5.1 Files needed

In order to have the circuit board manufactured, the data from the individual levels must be converted into a generally valid format. The Gerber format has established itself as the standard. It was developed in 1980 by Gerber Scientific to control photoplotters. It is in ASCII format. The x-y coordinates are defined in the format and what is to be done there. Only one level is described at a time. Which means we need multiple files to create the board.

In principle we always need:

- the Gerber files themselves
- drill files
- drill map files

Very important:

- Check compliance with the design rules (DRC check) before creating the files.
  All errors and warnings should be removed. Sometimes it's just a tiny piece of the wire that's forgotten to erase. However, the arrows point to the error location and the mouse over it often shows what is wrong.
- After creating the Gerber files you have to check them in the Gerber viewer.

5.2 Creation of the Gerber files

Since there are several files and the circuit board manufacturers do not want them individually, but as a packed (.zip) file, we first create an empty folder that we give a meaningful name (e.g. that of the project). We will later place all files in this folder and then compress the folder with the files it contains.

We call up the production data from the board editor and from there the Gerber files (*File → Fabrication Outputs → Gerbers (.gbr)*).

Chapter 5: Files for board manufacturer 59

The plotting window opens.

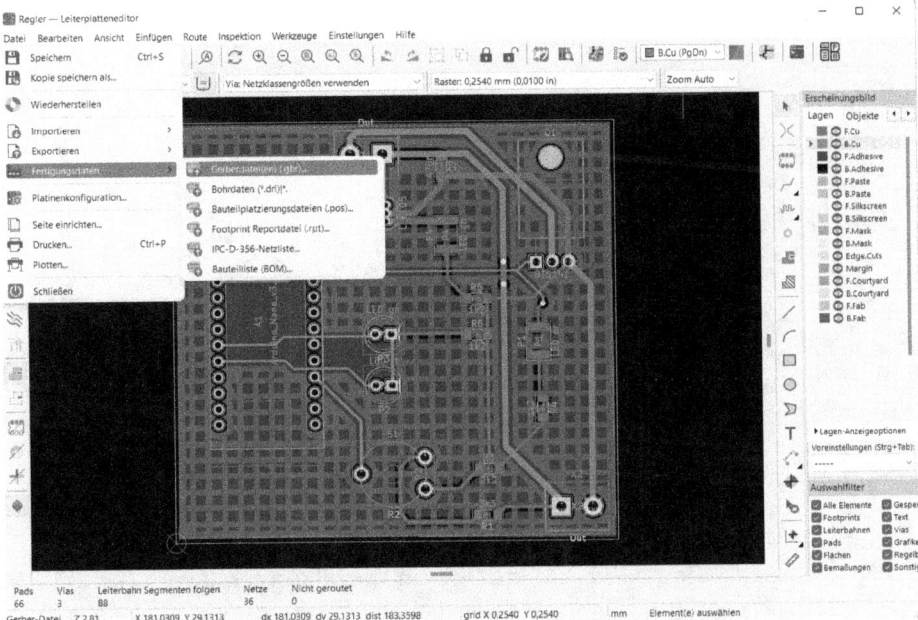

Fig. 48: Fabrication Outputs

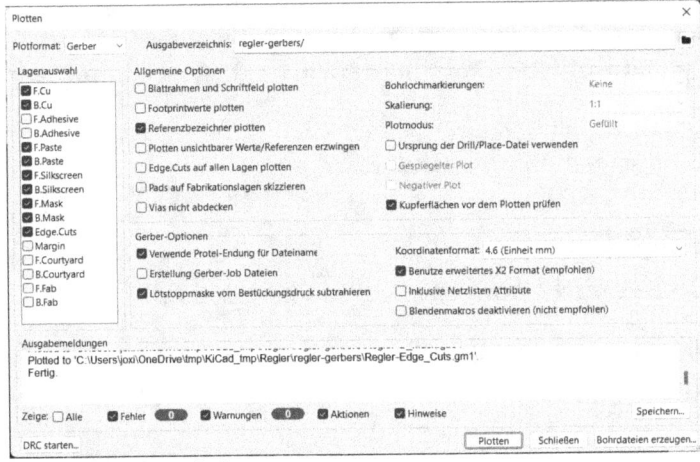

Fig. 49: Plotting window

Here we define what is to be putout on which level. Which exact parameters are activated depends on the board manufacturer. I am referring here to the company JLCPCB [4]. It's best to check the manufacturer's website to see if there are any special settings.

The following levels should be activated:

- F.Cu, B.Cu
- F.Paste, B.Paste
- F.Silkscreen, B.Silkscreen
- F.Mask, B.Mask
- Edge.Cuts

The directory in which the files are to be stored is selected at the top. If you don't do it, they are all in the project folder and you have to laboriously search for them. There is a risk of forgetting something or sorting out the wrong ones.

The options on the right mean:

- Plot reference designators
  Makes the identifiers (R1, C1, etc.) go on the silkscreen layer.

- Use Protel filename extensions
  The Protel company at the time had developed a program for creating printed circuit boards and defined endings in it. This manufacturer requires these endings - others may require others.

- Subtract soldermask from silkscreen
  This ensures that no screen printing takes place on pads.

- Check zone fills before plotting

- The X2 format can be switched on, but does not have to be.

Then hit *Plot* and leave the window open. If copper areas were created but not filled or not rebuilt after changes, there is an error message that prompts you to fill.

Now we create the drilling files. To do this, we click on *Generate Drill Files* at the bottom right.

The Gerber format is required. For oval holes, this provider requires the alternative drilling mode (*Use alternate drill mode*). At the top right we can see how many holes and vias there are. Both vias and pads are metallized and are therefore in contact with both sides of the board. The non-metallized pad is the mounting hole. The folder in which the file is to be stored is displayed at the top again.

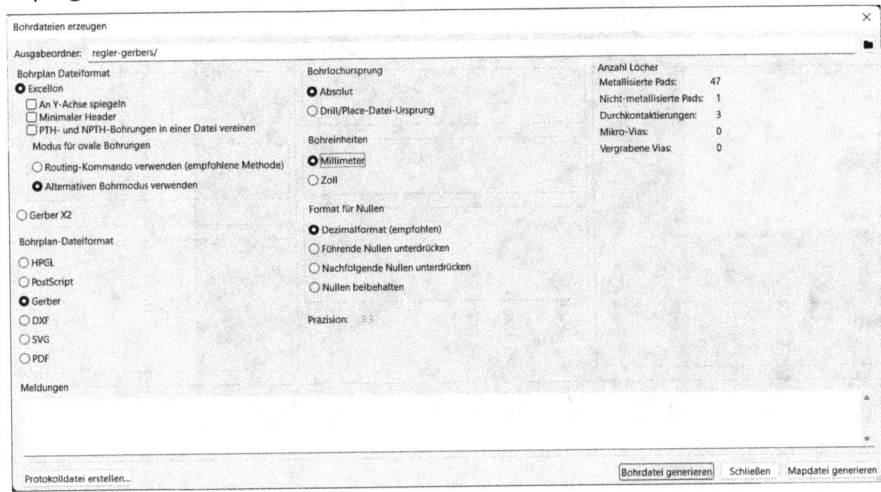

Fig. 50: Drill files

A click on *Generate Drill File* creates the drilling file. The map file is optional but recommended. Since it doesn't generate additional work, we generate it with it. After that we can close the windows.

We now go to the folder where the folder with the Gerber files is located. We compress this folder into a .zip file. We will later upload this file to the board manufacturer. But first, let's check them out. To do this, we open the Gerber viewer.

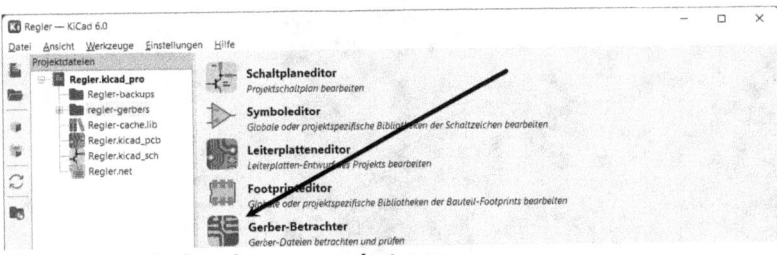

Fig. 51: Open Gerber viewer on project page

The empty viewer opens with many empty layers. In this we load the .zip file.

The created Gerber files appear above the existing layers and are displayed in the workspace.

Chapter 5: Files for board manufacturer

Fig. 52: Load packed file into Gerber viewer

Now you can look at the individual files. It is advisable to first switch off all newly added levels and then only look at one at a time. If you find errors (e.g. missing labeling that you may have placed on the wrong layer), you can

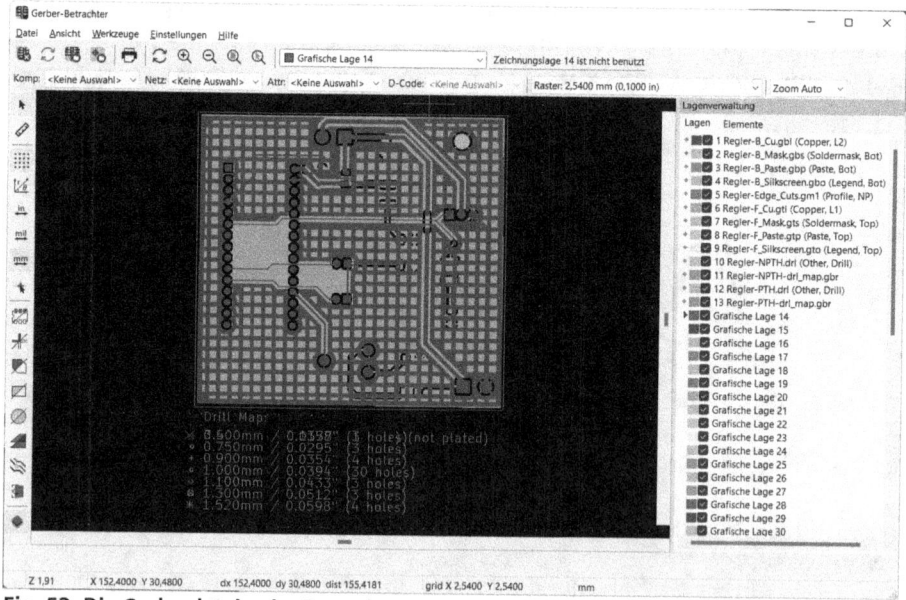

Fig. 53: Die Gerberdateien im Betrachter

change them in the board editor. Of course, the relevant Gerber file then has to be regenerated.

If everything is satisfactory, the .zip file can be uploaded to the board manufacturer.

6 References

[1] ...: Eagle im Hobbybereich. mikrocontroller.net.
[Online] https://www.mikrocontroller.net/articles/Eagle_im_Hobbybereich#Empfehlungen_für_Leiterbahnen_im_Hobbybereich
Stand: 21.04.2022

[2] Zickert, G.: Leiterplatten - Stromlaufplan, Layout und Fertigung. Fachbuchverlag Leipzig im Carl Hanser Verlag. 2. Auflage 2018

[3] ...: Platinenhersteller. mikrocontroller.net.
[Online] https://www.mikrocontroller.net/articles/Platinenhersteller
Stand: 08.05.2022

[4] ...: How to generate Gerber and Drill files in KiCad 6. jlcpcb.com.
[Online] https://support.jlcpcb.com/article/194-how-to-generate-gerber-and-drill-files-in-kicad-6
Stand: 09.05.2022

[5] Gustrau, F.; Kellerbauer, H.: Elektromagnetische Verträglichkeit. Fachbuchverlag Leipzig im Carl Hanser Verlag. 2015

[6] ...: KiCad. kicad.org.
[Online] https://www.kicad.org
Stand: 09.05.2022

7 Index

C
  Circuit symbols 27
  Components 11
    SMD 11
    THT 11
  configuration 15
  Connections 31

D
  Design Rules 45

E
  ERC check 35

F
  Filled zone 53
  Footprints 34
  FR2 10
  FR4 10

G
  Gate-Swapping 48

H
  heat traps 14

I
  Installation 15

M
  Mechanical component 52

P
  Pads 13
  PCB Editor 37

PCB Layers 43
Pin swapping 49
Placement of the components 11
Power connections 32
Printed circuit board 9
Project Manager 17

R
  Reference designator 33
  Routing 46

S
  Schematic Editor 23
  Symbol properties 29

T
  Template 21

Index

www.ingramcontent.com/pod-product-compliance
Lightning Source LLC
Chambersburg PA
CBHW070317220526
45465CB00004B/1881